I absolutely loved this book; I just wish it was written prior to my own divorce. Much of what Alexandra wrote truly resonated with me, and her candid and inspirational message would certainly be helpful to anyone else going through the divorce process. I have gotten to know this author by following her on Instagram, and she certainly does walk the walk and not just talk the talk. Her growth from her experiences is clearly evident by the positive life she is living now, but she also keeps it real by talking about the good, the bad, and the ugly. In doing so, Alexandra is undoubtedly providing a lot of help for many readers and followers. If you are contemplating divorce or in the midst of one, this book is a must-read to have in your tool kit to help in the healing process and in moving forward to live your best life. Alexandra's book exemplifies the fact that a divorce does not signify the end of your life, but the beginning of one.

Nadine Haruni, Author of The Freeda the Frog™ Children's Book Series
IG @freedathefrog www.freedathefrog.com

Alexandra's gripping tale of divorce and its aftermath is the perfect guide for any woman struggling with moving on. Not only is Alexandra's journey inspirational, but the interactive exercises are sure to propel anyone into a much better place and happier next chapter of their life. I highly recommend giving this book a whirl!

Tiffany Ann Beverlin, CEO / Founder DreamsRecycled.com
IG @DreamsRecyled www.DreamsRecycled.com

Alexandra was on my show *The Dude Therapist* and shared such powerful, honest, and real tips and tools when it comes to handling the new life post-divorce.

This book is just as amazing and more!

It brings truth and vulnerability to a very hard topic and times in people's lives.

This is a must-read for all those who have or are currently going through the journey of divorce. You won't regret reading it!

Eli Weinstein, LCSW
IG @eliweinstein_lcsw and @thedudetherapist www.eliweinsteinlcsw.com

Her Awakening is a profoundly moving and inspiring story of one woman's journey through the life-changing event of divorce. As someone who has practised family law for two decades, I have no doubt that Alexandra's beautiful and authentic account of her journey will help those who are navigating separation or divorce feel less alone and more empowered to rise from their experience and embrace their future.

Anita Volikis, family lawyer, author, certified coach
IG @anitavolikis www.anitavolikis.com

ALEXANDRA EVA-MAY

HER
Awakening

ONE WOMAN'S **JOURNEY** **TO HEALING** AFTER DIVORCE

Lauren,
It's been so lovely being
Friends these past few years!
Thank you so much for
supporting my work! ♡
alexandra
Eva-may

YGTMEDIA COMPANY

TORONTO

Published in Canada, for Global Distribution by YGTMedia Co.

www.ygtmedia.co/publishing

To order additional copies of this book: publishing@ygtmedia.co

Developmental Editing by Tania Jane Moraes-Vaz

Edited by Christine Stock

Book design by Doris Chung

Cover design by Michelle Fairbanks

ePub & Kindle editions by Ellie Silpa

Printed in North America

Dedicated to those who are brave enough to step into the unknown.

Table of Contents

ONE

Confronting
THE INITIAL SHOCK

I stood on the front steps of my parents' house for quite some time. I was preparing myself to share the news that my marriage had just ended and my entire world had broken into a million tiny pieces.

Thinking back to that day, I honestly was terrified. It felt like my universe had been destroyed and the very ground I stood on had exploded from under my feet.

I had no idea what to do. I felt helpless.

Even though I was a primary participant in the destruction and dissolution of my marriage, I couldn't believe what was happening. Shock and disbelief flooded my brain. I wasn't ready to face the reality of what was happening. I didn't know what to do. I didn't know where to look for solace. Everything was dark.

I remember how it took all my strength and courage to drive myself to my parents' home. Beyond that, I'm surprised I had the capacity to do anything else. I had no idea how I was going to share with them that my marriage was over.

It was one of those moments you read about in books or see in movies, and now, this moment was my reality. I never thought *I* would experience it. I could barely believe it was happening. I had no idea how to accept my current reality or what I was going to say about it. I was filled with so much worry that the conversation ahead of me was about to shatter two more hearts. I didn't know if I could do that to my parents.

My mother was raised Catholic. As a child, she attended Mass every Sunday. Throughout her life, faith has guided her values and beliefs. My parents continued in the Catholic tradition by raising me and my siblings as Catholics. Some of my earliest memories are of my family attending Mass together. I remember myself as a child, in the pew, doing my best to sit still and listen to the priest. I remember every single Christmas Eve Mass and all the sacraments I received. We were taught Catholic values and attended Catholic schools. I even became a Catholic school teacher. And when it came time to get married, it was a given that I would marry in the church. And that's just what I did.

The man I married is Ukrainian Catholic. When it was time to plan our wedding, we attended marriage prep at the church and planned a Catholic ceremony. On a beautiful day in July, we said our vows and made promises in front of our family and friends, and also God.

It was a wonderful day, and the church was gorgeous. In fact, it is probably one of the most special churches in my whole city, being that it's the only Basilica there, and it is the church where Wayne Gretzky said his vows. If you know anything about Edmonton, Canada, and hockey, you probably have heard about Gretzky's Stanley Cup winning stretch as an Edmonton Oiler back in the 1980s. So, to be married in the same place as he was is something to be proud of as an Edmontonian! That Basilica was also the church where my parents said their wedding vows. I'm sure this fact added to their pride on my wedding day.

More important than their daughter getting married in the same church as they did, however, was that I was joining so many of my relatives who were already members of the marriage club. Within my extended family, marriage is a big trend. There have been a lot of weddings and a lot of kids. And after the initial vows, people in my family don't typically divorce. Among all my grandparents, aunts, uncles, and cousins, there are very few divorces. Unfortunately, with the end of my marriage, I was about to make that number a bit larger.

Getting back to the scene.

There I was, standing on the front steps of my parents' home, tears in my eyes and with a bag of clothes slung over my shoulder, contemplating how I was going to tell my Catholic family that their Catholic daughter was doing one of the most uncatholic things a Catholic can do—getting a divorce.

In reflection, my announcement came out exactly the way that tragic news usually does: suddenly and all at once. Shaking, scared, and unsure, I broke the news: "Mom, my marriage is over."

That's where this whole journey started—a journey that has been the most transformative venture of my life.

Don't be afraid to stand alone and rediscover who you are.

TWO

Ten Lessons
I LEARNED FROM THE END OF MY MARRIAGE

After confessing my separation to my parents, the remainder of the night was filled with me explaining how everything had fallen apart. _Who? What? When? Where? Why? How?_ Hours were spent talking about what went wrong and what had happened. I remember the look in my mom's eyes when I laid everything on the line. It was a mix of surprise, pain, and heartbreak. I don't blame her. I can't imagine it was easy to hear.

During the whole conversation, I felt numb. Out of body, yet present. At the same time, that conversation was pivotal in my journey. It was there that I finally let go of so many things I had held in for so long. Up until that point, there were so many details about what had been happening in the marriage that I hadn't shared with anyone. It felt good to finally open up. It was extremely therapeutic.

After everything was said and done, it was decided that I would live with my parents for a while.

Mom took me downstairs to my childhood bedroom. I dropped my bag and sat in silence. My whole life had just exploded, and I had no idea what I was going to do or how I was going to survive. But here I was, comforted that at least my childhood room was still the same. It was the one constant in my life right then, apart from my parents. At that moment, it was hard not to feel emotional.

All at once, the energy of the room washed over me. I was reminded of all the beautiful memories that had happened there. This room was where I had grown up. Junior high sleepovers. High school hangouts, laughing with my best friend. It was there where I disclosed secrets to my diary and imagined how my happy future would look. I can promise you I never once pictured divorce as part of my future.

Yet, there I was, facing exactly that, and I was a puddle. I couldn't hold back the tears. I cried not only for the girl who had spent her childhood expecting her life to be filled with only joy but also for the woman whose life was now in pieces.

When I look back on that night, I wish I could give that grief-stricken woman an enormous hug. I wish I could tell her that everything would be okay. More than that, I wish I could tell her that everything, after traveling the hard road ahead, will be sensational.

I wish I could give my former self a play-by-play of what would happen over the next few years, to prepare her for what was coming. I wish I could warn my younger self that I was about to face my own personal hell—that the pain would hit like nothing I'd ever felt before. I wish I could tell my younger self that suffering is part of the healing process. That sometimes we have to fumble and stumble in our life's journey and live unconsciously until we awaken to consciousness. That many times the journey will feel hard, unbearable even, but it is awakening you to who you are meant to become. More than anything, though, I wish I could tell my younger self that at the end of it all, life will be magnificent. I wish I could properly explain that the greatest adventures happen after starting over with nothing.

It would be foolish to go through a divorce (a huge life-changing experience) and not learn invaluable, life-altering lessons. My divorce happened when I was a relatively young age, which presented a unique opportunity to learn these lessons earlier than I would have had I not gone through it.

In all honesty, I'm not sure I would have learned these lessons at any point in my life if I hadn't gone through the end of my marriage.

Divorce ripped me to pieces. My consequent descent into a dark depression almost destroyed anything that was left. Losing so much left me feeling like I had absolutely nothing remaining, when, in fact, the entire experience stirred something deep in my soul and shifted the course of my entire life.

My divorce had to happen at exactly the time it happened to get me to where I am now and to direct where I'm going. The lessons that my divorce taught me changed me indefinitely and will serve me forever. I wouldn't be the person I am today without these lessons, and I'm eternally thankful.

When I started writing this book, I knew I wanted to share these lessons early on. I look at it this way: knowing these truths would have helped me accept the pain and grief more easily and would have helped me so much along the way.

I'm going to do for you what I wish someone had done for me. I'm going to share the lessons I learned throughout my journey to help inspire healing and acceptance in you, right now.

Lesson #1 BEING SINGLE IS SIGNIFICANTLY BETTER THAN BEING IN A MARRIAGE THAT EATS AWAY AT YOUR SPIRIT.

During my marriage, it didn't take long for the tides of unhappiness to set in. The relentless, unsettling, horrible feeling that my marriage was not right was all-consuming. My mental health plummeted, and I was desperate.

After the marriage ended and I survived the consequent grief, I gained a new appreciation for the bliss that is *single-dom*. I started to feel lighter, more at peace, and happy. Days were brighter, and I was hopeful. Life was better.

There's a lot of joy to be found in the adventure that follows the end of a marriage. You get to rediscover exactly who you are, without any influence from a partner. You get to spend quality time falling in love with yourself all over again. It's really an amazing opportunity to achieve true happiness and to deepen your self-love and self-trust.

It may seem impossible now, but in the long run, you'll be significantly happier alone (if that is, in fact, how life pans out) rather than in a marriage that doesn't serve you. At the same time, it is important to note that the likelihood of you being alone forever is slim.

Either way, no relationship is worth your well-being. Period.

Lesson #2 THERE'S NOTHING LIKE A FAILED MARRIAGE TO BUILD TRUE RESILIENCY.

Want to understand the human capacity for resiliency? Put a bunch of divorcées together in one room. They'll teach you a thing or two about picking yourself up off the floor, pushing on when it seems impossible, and eventually thriving.

Divorce is a heart-crushing event, to say the least. It's devastating, stressful, painful, and life altering. There are so many moments when you just want to give up and live in your pain; however, sometimes, it is the heartbreaks in life that are exactly what we need to help us transform. For even the most positive, optimistic person, to survive a divorce, you must develop a brand-new set of coping skills. I had to learn how to heal my broken heart. I had to learn how to ignite my darkened spirit. I had to learn how to get back on my feet financially. I had to learn how to face life alone without the comfort of a relationship. Essentially, I had to learn how to live life on my own terms without the reassurance of anyone else.

Because I was able to survive my own divorce, I can better deal with disappointment. I'm calmer when struggle comes my way. I know things will ultimately be all right because I got through the one experience I thought would destroy me. I am now confident that I can cope with anything that comes my way.

Lesson #3 I CAN THRIVE ALL ON MY OWN.

Prior to my divorce, I had spent my entire adult life in one relationship or another. I was like Liz in the movie *Eat, Pray, Love* when she explained, "Since I was fifteen, I've either been with a guy or breaking up with a guy. I haven't had so much as two weeks just to deal with myself."

Like Liz, I had never really stood on my own two feet. I was always dating, in relationships, or depending on someone else. I had relied on the men in my life to take care of me and had never truly learned how to love myself all on my own or to support myself.

In the initial months after my divorce, I struggled so much just to exist as a single person. Sleeping alone was a struggle. Attending social events by myself caused anxiety. There were many moments when my new independent life seemed impossible.

I remember one time, just after the marriage ended, when my complete lack of independence smacked me in the face. I was driving to the movie theater to meet some friends when the cops pulled me over. I was speeding. Not by much, but enough to get pulled over. When the officer asked for my insurance and registration, I realized that my registration was outdated, and my insurance card wasn't in the car. There I was, over the speed limit, with no registration and no insurance card to be found.

The officer explained to me that he had grounds to give me more than $2,000 in fines. I desperately searched for documents but couldn't find anything. Being completely overwhelmed, I broke down in tears, and not the manipulative, get-out-of-a-ticket tears. These were real, I-can't-handle-anything-right-and-I-don't-know-how-to-cope tears.

So, how did I end up in this situation? Well, my ex had taken care of car things. And before him, it had been my dad. Heck, I hadn't even put air in my tires on my own. When my ex and I split, it was right around the time when the insurance and registration needed to be done.

Through my sobs, I explained it all to the officer. "I'm getting a divorce, and I've never done this stuff before. I've never registered my car before. I didn't know I had to. I know that's not an excuse, but it's my reality."

I think if I hadn't been crying so much, he probably would have been annoyed with my ignorance and slapped the $2,000 ticket in my lap. However, I'm sure he saw I was hurting and was being genuine. He let me go with a warning, told me to take care of it as soon as possible, and pointed me in the direction of the closest registries.

Thankfully, because of this situation, I quickly figured out all the car requirements that I now had to do on my own. Slowly, I also figured everything else out. Through different experiences and the passage of time, I was able to not only embrace life as a single woman but also to kick ass as my new single self.

Since my divorce, I'm now in a place where I feel fully confident in my ability to function in the world as an independent person. I don't need anyone to do anything for me. I can manage just fine by myself. The period of independence and self-love has been liberating!

Lesson #4   YOUR FRIENDS AND FAMILY JUST WANT YOU TO BE HAPPY.

When you announce your divorce, friends and family will be surprised, sad, and disappointed. The initial shock of your split will have ripple effects among your relatives and your social groups.

Thankfully, it won't last forever.

When I told people about my divorce, reactions were mixed. Most people were shocked and saddened. Some people were immediately supportive, while others told me I should "try harder." (I will get to all the unsolicited advice I received during my divorce in a later chapter because the same might just happen to you.)

There may be people who question your decision. Some friends may even abandon you. Honestly, those aren't the people who deserve to be in your life. People who truly love you just want you to be happy. If there is someone in your life who doesn't see your happiness as a priority, you should do yourself (and them) a favor and back away from that friendship.

You deserve to prioritize personal joy more than anyone who questions your decision.

You'll quickly realize that loved ones just want to see you smiling and thriving. Friends and family will rally around you and support you through this season of transition in your life. You'll also realize that people are generally far too concerned with themselves and their own problems to give you and your life that much attention. People will move on and adjust relatively quickly to your single status.

Lesson #5 — DIVORCE CREATES NEW FRIENDSHIPS AND CONNECTIONS YOU NEVER EXPECTED.

Divorce is a foreign experience to anyone who hasn't experienced it and can feel alienating if you don't have family or friends who've lived through it. Throughout this process, you'll ultimately seek out connections with fellow divorcées because they can identify with you and your experience. If you are anything like me, these new friendships might become some of your nearest and dearest.

Some of my closest friendships were formed after I separated from my ex. The universe brought other divorcées into my sphere, and we connected in a way that was paramount to my healing. One of my best friendships was formed after my divorce.

If I hadn't experienced divorce, I don't think I would have developed these friendships, which were the exact relationships my soul needed. The light created by these bonds has helped me grow into the person I'm becoming.

Lesson #6 — I HAVE THINGS TO WORK ON TO BE A BETTER PARTNER.

Early in the divorce process, it was easy to play the blame game. In my mind, there was a constant stream of *It was his fault! He did this! He did that!*

After countless hours of therapy and self-reflection, I realized there were aspects of myself that I needed to work on to be a better partner in a relationship. I also realized that I contributed to the demise of my marriage more than I originally thought. If I ever hoped to be in a healthy relationship, there was so much I needed to do.

I had to find my voice and work on standing up for myself. I had to develop confidence that someone would still love me even if I spoke my mind and shared things they didn't want to hear or weren't ready to hear. I had to develop my communication skills, not just with intimate partners, but with everyone in my life. I had to learn how to create boundaries and act accordingly if someone overstepped those boundaries. I had to learn how to stand up to toxic interactions in relationships. I had to figure out how to not lose myself in a relationship.

Essentially, I had to learn to love myself first.

That statement isn't as selfish as it sounds. What it means is that I had to learn how to prioritize my needs first and to respect myself, above all. It was the only way I would ever be any good for anyone else.

And it would come with time. It would be evident in every single interaction I had post-divorce. Every sacred yes and no I leaned into.

Every boundary I upheld. Every interaction when I showed up with love—for myself first, which then flowed to others.

If I had stayed married, I never would have taken such a hard look at my behaviors. I would have continued to repeat old patterns and would have never truly changed in the ways I needed to in order to have a successful relationship. Honestly, I probably would have ended up divorced one way or another at some point in my life. Divorce forced me to take a long, hard look at myself and start to work on things that I desperately needed to improve.

Lesson #7   THERE ARE WAY MORE FISH IN THE SEA OR BIRDS IN THE SKY (OR ANY OTHER ANIMAL/NATURE IDIOM YOU'D LIKE TO USE).

There are billions of people on this earth. The idea that there isn't someone else out there for you is absurd! Your ex isn't the only person on this planet you can love who is ready to love you to pieces.

Even more ludicrous is the notion that there isn't someone even better suited for you than your ex. I'm going to give you the piece of advice that my sister told me early on during my divorce: "There will be a person in your future who will love you more than you ever imagined."

By ending your marriage, you have perhaps made the necessary space for an even more perfect partner to enter the scene.

When you're plagued by regret and you are missing your ex, know this: When we think about failed relationships, we often recall only the happy memories. There's a reason why you chose to get divorced. It wasn't all happy. In fact, for many of you, it was probably downright miserable. You deserve more than that! Remind yourself of this fact every time you want to go back down memory lane and recall *only* the happy memories.

You deserve to smile from ear to ear. You deserve to feel fulfilled and at peace. You deserve to feel calm and appreciated. You deserve to love fully with every piece of yourself and feel extremely loved and valued in return. You deserve to feel seen, heard, valued, and felt in your relationship.

You deserve to feel joy every day.

There's possibly going to be someone amazing in your future who'll be exactly right for you, and that future someone could love you more deeply than you ever imagined and will change your perspective on love.

And if that relationship doesn't work, on to the next!

Lesson #8 MY FIRST MARRIAGE WAS ONLY ONE CHAPTER IN MY LIFE.

Sometimes, we can be extremely short-sighted when thinking about our lives. The past, present, and very limited future may be all we see. Many of us find it hard to see beyond the current reality or the short-term future. It's almost easier to think about the pain, stress, and hardship of right now instead of imagining what we want our lives to look and feel like in the future.

Many divorcées experience enormous difficulty when finally ending their marriage because of regret and uncertainty. Adjusting to single life after so many years with someone can feel challenging, no matter the reason for ending the union. And ending a union that you know is going to fail in the long run is exactly the right choice.

Marriage is an agreement that's supposed to last the rest of your life. If you're this unhappy right now, imagine what it might be like twenty years from today if you stayed married. Let that sit with you for a while whenever you feel any sort of regret.

Now is the time to give yourself credit. You've made a very important decision to not settle for an unhappy existence. More so, you've taken the first step to create space in your life to welcome a conscious partnership. You've cleared the path ahead of you so that you can start walking the path you're destined to be on.

There's a very fulfilling life that's waiting for you. You were meant to close your marriage chapter so that you can open new doors. You are meant to walk a different path. You are meant to get going on your incredible journey and discover the life you're destined to live.

Your story isn't over. You're just getting started. Keep going!

Lesson #9 "FAILURE" OPENS NEW DOORS.

If you look at divorce through a black-and-white lens, it's no question that it signifies failure. Additionally, we still live in sociocultural contexts that perpetuate this norm. There are far too many people who stay in unhealthy, toxic marriages because they made vows to each other, God, and their community. And often, it's also because we are worried about what others might think of us. Add children into the mix, and now you've really got yourself a game of socio-cultural and emotional Russian Roulette. However, it's important to remember that it is a marriage that failed to fulfill the promises that either one or both individuals made to each other—the promises to last until death, to love, value, cherish, and be kind no matter what failed on a basic level, which is why you chose to end it. And ending a marriage that only brings forth unhappiness isn't a failure. Not even a little bit. Choosing to divorce is choosing to prioritize your happiness, self-worth, value, and self-love.

Any choice born out of self-love can't be a failure, even if it's a divorce.

The end of a marriage is a significant opportunity to reshape your life to be whatever you want. It's the promise of new possibilities. It's a time when you can create a beautiful life just for you.

You can book that trip you've always dreamed about, change jobs, or embark on a brand-new career altogether. You are free to move cities, embrace new friendships, seek out new love, or pursue hobbies you've always wanted to discover. You finally have the space to be whoever you want and embrace yourself fully without any kind of reservation. You are free to learn about and anchor deeply into being who you are.

Since the end of my marriage, I discovered my love of writing, learned how to create and manage a successful blog, connected with people all over the world, traveled to multiple continents, wrote a book, and healed my soul in the most beautiful way. I've been blessed with so many gifts, and I feel incredibly lucky every single day. You have no idea about the opportunities that exist following this so-called *failure*.

Lesson #10   I'M WORTHY OF AN INCREDIBLE LIFE!

The most important lesson I learned after my marriage ended is that I won't settle for unhappiness or mediocrity. That is the standard I've set for my life, and I'll forever seek it out in all that I do. I refuse to settle for anything less.

I should feel accepted, even at my worst. I deserve to feel peace and light. I deserve to feel emotionally safe and loved beyond measure.

Repeat this mantra with me:

I'm worthy of healthy love.

I'm worthy of acceptance.

I'm worthy of peace.

I'm worthy of joy.

Most importantly, I'm worthy of a sensationally extraordinary life that makes me smile with my whole heart.

And you're just as worthy.

You're Going to Make It.

During my separation and divorce, journaling was a saving grace. Writing helped me release the hidden thoughts and emotions that I had pushed deep in my soul (that I didn't want to tell anyone).

I couldn't talk about what I was thinking and feeling, so writing in a journal was the next best thing.

Journaling helped me start prioritizing my mental health. The mere act of writing my thoughts and emotions on paper helped release the grip they had on my mind.

At the end of each chapter, there is a writing exercise to help you usher in some serious healing.

Jot down any feelings or thoughts that arise (no matter how dark or depressing). Scribble down any discoveries you make about yourself that can help cultivate light in your life.

It doesn't matter if it's just words strung together. It doesn't matter if it is in point form. It doesn't matter if you write an entire chapter yourself.

This act of writing will help you grow and, more importantly, heal.

Your Task

Write down the top ten lessons you learned from the end of your marriage.

Maybe your lessons are the same as mine and perhaps they're entirely different. It doesn't matter one bit! Just get writing. This activity is all for you!

Even if it doesn't seem like it, you're on track. Any adversity you're experiencing is teaching you lessons that will help you evolve. Any hardship you're facing is cultivating strength you will need in the future. You're currently becoming exactly who you're destined to be.

THREE

Get Yourself
TO THERAPY RIGHT NOW

The first time I considered therapy was following a suggestion from a friend after I confided in her about my grief. Therapy had helped her, and she thought I could benefit from it.

I had never gone to therapy before and didn't have a good impression of it. In my limited understanding, I believed therapy wasn't something for me. *I can get through this grief on my own,* I blindly believed. Well, that ridiculous thinking didn't last long. All it took was one more night of crying myself to sleep to realize that maybe I needed help with my grief.

The word *therapy* evokes many different reactions from people, and it really depends on your audience. Those who've never been to therapy probably have a completely different perception than those who make it a priority in their lives. It is also an experience that is unique to each person. If you have two people who have attended therapy, the value they place on the practice and their experiences will differ.

The words *patient* and *client* are traditionally used to describe individuals who seek help from a licensed therapist or counselor. I'm not entirely sure what word I feel most comfortable using. The label *patient* shows how important it is to care for our mental health to ensure holistic health, while the label *client* shows how therapeutic services are not necessarily seen as a necessity by all. Either way, my difficulty to select a word for the therapy "goer" drives home my point. Therapy is misunderstood by many, loved by others, and is a service that isn't used nearly enough by the majority.

Walking into the waiting room at my first appointment, I was a mess of confusion, untangled anxiety, and worry. I didn't know what to expect. I sat down and couldn't turn off my busy brain.

Will I be lying on one of those couches like I'd seen in the movies? Will I have anything to talk about? What if there are awkward silences? What if she judges me? What if she tells me I am wasting her time? Am I taking away time from people who need therapy more than I do? What if I don't belong here at all? What if someone finds out I am going to therapy? Will they understand? What if therapy doesn't work and just makes everything worse?

My therapist came out, greeted me, and told me to follow her into her office. Once inside, I noticed a bookshelf filled with different self-help books. Therapeutic tools were propped on shelves or on tables around the room. There were different pieces of furniture I could sit or lie down on. I made a beeline for the large red sofa by the window.

There I was, a therapy virgin, comfortably seated on a beautiful couch, sitting across from my first therapist, Sarah. She was warm and comforting, yet neutral in her facial expressions.

She started the first session by asking why I had come to see her. I remember answering very bluntly. "I don't know how to cope," I said with tears welling up in my eyes.

Sarah met this admission with acceptance and understanding, asking more questions about what was going on in my life. She never pushed when I couldn't answer a question. She didn't judge anything that was said in that room. Tears were welcomed and silences weren't uncomfortable.

I explained my issues and experiences as best as I could: the failure of my marriage and my inability to cope with what I was going through. I spoke about my grief, stress, anxiety, heartbreak, and everything else in between. All the while, Sarah listened. At the end of that first session, she provided me with a home exercise and recommended two books for me to read: *Broken Open: How Difficult*

Times Can Help Us Grow by Elizabeth Lesser and *Living Beautifully with Uncertainty and Change* by Pema Chödrön.

I left feeling better than when I had arrived. I felt lighter and like a burden had been lifted off my heart. I had work to do—I had that home exercise, after all, and a couple books to read, but that was just the beginning. The work I really had to do would be a process that would last three years. It was my own personal journey to heal.

I kept going back to therapy under the guidance of Sarah. Sometimes, I visited frequently, close to once a week, while other times, I was comfortable seeing her once a month. Most sessions, I walked away with new coping strategies to add to my personal tool kit, some sort of home exercise, and a book recommendation.

More than that, I walked away from each session feeling like I had unloaded a bit of the massive weight I carried inside my heart. I had so many feelings and thoughts that were incredibly damaging to my spirit and mental health. They weighed on me, and I felt suffocated.

Before I started therapy, there was never any release. Everything remained trapped and hidden inside. With therapy, I found my release. I could finally unload everything onto another person who gladly took on that weight, while treating me with ultimate kindness, compassion, and support. In that room, I never once felt judged or rejected. All I ever felt was love.

My therapist helped me heal in a way I never would have on my own.

I love therapy and believe it is for everyone! It's an hour of time when you talk about any problems, big or small. You can hash out complex emotions, discuss issues, work through stresses, communicate worries, and bare your soul. A good therapist will listen, empathize, and understand. They are bound by confidentiality obligations, so you don't have to worry about anything being repeated. It's an ideal scenario in which you can release thoughts and feelings.

You don't need a significant reason to attend therapy. In my opinion, it should be part of your larger self-care routine, something that is especially true for people who've been through life-altering experiences like divorce. The transition can be gut wrenching, and the trauma doesn't necessarily heal itself. The grief you feel during your divorce can be crippling. For many, it's not easy to heal after divorce.

A professional therapist is most likely necessary to help you work through everything you are thinking and feeling right now. Just like you wouldn't winterize a car without the help of a mechanic, you shouldn't enter a new season in your life without the help of a trained specialist: your therapist.

Different Kinds of Therapy

There are many types of therapies that you can explore. I'm not going to list or explain them all, but I'll address a few that may be helpful. If you're interested in the route I took, which was talk therapy (sometimes referred to as counseling), you'll be in a room with a psychologist for an hour or so, talking in confidence. This therapy is aimed at releasing complex emotions and thoughts you have difficulty working through on your own. Talk therapy can come in the form of one-on-one, in-person therapy (like I did). You could also have a session over the phone, through video conferencing, or over different apps. You might also opt for talk therapy in a group setting, which may be more comfortable.

You can also look into cognitive behavioral therapy (CBT). This type of therapy will help you explore and change how you think about your life. Cognitive behavioral therapy works to free you from unhelpful patterns of behavior. You'll set goals with your therapist and may be required to carry out tasks between sessions. This therapy is aimed at behavior changes to address personal habits and behavior patterns.

You may also wish to explore mindfulness-based cognitive therapy where you focus on thoughts and feelings that happen, moment by moment. This type of therapy will combine a variety of mindfulness techniques such as meditation and breathing exercises. This type of therapy may be one that you explore near the end of your healing journey to help you cope with staying on the course of mental wellness in your future.

If none of these speak to you, there are other therapies you can explore. I recommend you do a bit of research to find what you believe will work best for you and go from there.

Choosing the Right Therapist

Finding a therapist is relatively simple. You can go online and search for therapists in your city, ask friends and family for referrals, check out local blogs, search social media, or read a newspaper for listings. It may also be wise to contact the Human Resources representative in your workplace to see if there is a specific therapist that is covered by medical benefits. There is a wide variety of avenues that can lead to many different therapists.

Even though it can be easy enough to *find* a therapist, the real challenge is finding the *right* therapist for *you*.

Let me paint a picture of what happens to a lot of people. Let's say you've finally convinced yourself to invest in therapy. You're excited because your therapy journey is about to begin! You spend time looking on the internet and asking for referrals. You eventually find a therapist that seems like a good fit, and you book an appointment.

Unfortunately, once the session starts, you feel like you aren't seeing eye-to-eye with the person seated across from you. You find yourself thinking, *This person doesn't get me.* When you walk out of the appointment, you doubt the whole process and convince yourself it isn't for you. Right then and there, you decide to never go back to therapy.

When I say this situation happens to a lot of people, I'm not exaggerating. There are so many people who walk away from their first therapy appointment feeling let down because the appointment didn't live up to their expectations. Many people make the mistake of assuming their first experience with therapy is indicative of every experience they might have, which leads them to give up on the practice entirely, something that breaks my heart because it just isn't true.

The idea that all therapy and all therapists are alike is completely and totally false. Every therapist has different experiences, educational backgrounds, and interests. They have different specialties and focuses. One therapist may have an exorbitant amount of relationship knowledge, while another is an expert in the field of grief and loss. Communication style is as varied between therapists as it is between people. You may mesh extremely well with one therapist and find another one quite brash and unlikable.

Choosing a therapist that is right for you can be a process.

It can take a while to find someone you feel comfortable with and with whom you believe understands what you're experiencing. You shouldn't swear off therapy just because you have one bad experience. You shouldn't swear off therapy even if you've had five bad experiences.

It is very possible you just haven't found the right therapist for you. If the first one didn't quite mesh with you, book an appointment with someone else. If that one doesn't work out, try someone else. Give it a real try. Don't give up. If you swear off therapy after a few failed sessions with therapists you feel aren't right, it could take you much longer to heal.

Even If You Are Nervous, Give Yourself this Gift

If you're like I was and feeling hesitant to seek out therapy for yourself, trust me, it's completely normal. Do your best to move through your fear. You have no idea how helpful it can be in your journey to heal unless you try.

I firmly believe that therapy is important for anyone experiencing a serious transition in their life, especially when coping with the transition that follows the end of a marriage. There are about a million emotions that can spring up while coping with divorce. Your grief may feel overwhelming. There could be trauma that you're dealing with following your split. You could be facing extreme feelings of loss and shame, all which might require a professional in mental health to help you heal.

You wouldn't try to get through a major physical trauma, like a broken leg, without the help of a doctor. Thus, you shouldn't try to get through major heartbreak without the help of a professional.

If you decide to commit to therapy, you're very likely to develop coping skills so that you'll be able to move through challenging times like a warrior, discover things about yourself you never knew, uncover unresolved traumas, and identify relationship patterns and general patterns in behavior that may be detrimental to your wellness.

More so, therapy helps lighten the heavy load that you've been carrying in your heart. It is a safe space to talk through stress, anxiety, trauma, fear, grief, and any other complex emotions with a professional who is there to listen to and support you. You are free to bare your soul, share your heartbreak, and reveal any shame or loneliness you feel. It's a safe space to finally let everything go that you've been holding in for so long.

Give yourself this gift.

You're Going to Make It.

Your Task

Create a 4-step plan

1. Make a plan for how you can make therapy a reality in your life.

2. Write down the type of therapy you want to try first.

3. Jot down the issues you think therapy could help you work through.

4. Write down what you would like to discuss with a therapist.

Divorce creates a space to grow into your most beautiful self.

FOUR

Coping
WITH LONELINESS

The loneliness after divorce can be suffocating. The trauma and loss you've experienced has most likely left wounds that are still healing. I know this because I went through it.

When my marriage fell apart, I found myself suddenly single and helplessly lonely. I was without *my person*. The space that used to be filled by my husband and my marriage was now filled with emptiness and solitude. Just existing day to day seemed impossible.

Yes, I chose divorce; however, that did not mean I was immune from missing my ex or immune from feeling incredibly lonely. I shared a life with someone. We built memories together. Even during the fights and hardships, we still had each other. No one will ever know what went on in my marriage behind closed doors or truly understand the relationship I had with my ex. Initially, losing my spouse left a huge gaping hole, and it was really difficult to fill that void.

One of the biggest misconceptions about divorce is that those who go through it don't miss their ex. For me, this belief was untrue. Even though I knew divorce was the healthiest path for me, there were so many moments when I missed my ex and felt tragically alone.

I knew that divorce was the only answer, but I missed him, every single day, for a really long time. I missed his presence. I missed his sense of humor. I missed his love of Pearl Jam. I missed his laugh. I missed his smile. I missed going on trips together. I missed our talks. I missed our shows. I missed going to concerts together. I missed his family. I missed my best friend, and I missed our life.

Sometimes, I felt like the loneliest person on the planet. I felt like I'd never escape the loneliness and that I'd be alone forever.

At times, it felt insufferable.

What's even worse is that I hid my loneliness from others. A big mistake I made early in the divorce process was that I isolated myself from the people I loved. I was so lonely, yet I chose to remain alone a lot of the time. When I went through episodes of loneliness, the last thing I wanted to do was invite anyone into my dark reality. I believed that revealing my pain to others would be a burden for them. If you can relate, I see you. It's normal to want to shut everyone out, and truthfully, there are some people you absolutely must shut out (think naysayers and unsupportive friends or family members). But for the love of yourself and your sanity, let a few trusted souls in. During the process, it was easy for me to shut everyone out. It felt safer to guard myself and put up walls. When someone reached out and tried to join in on my loneliness journey, I found it really difficult to let them travel alongside me.

My solution was to put on masks and hide my grief. Isolation seemed like a safe choice. I actively went out of my way to avoid social gatherings, turned down invitations, and spent weekends alone in my house. This isolation ended up being a terrible course of action, however, because loneliness hit harder when I shut everyone out. My self-created isolation extended my suffering and only further fueled my darkness.

Eventually, being alone with my pain was too much. I needed to release some of it. When I finally opened up to those around me, I learned an extremely important lesson. **Don't prolong your darkness further. Navigating the dark with a few trusted loved ones beats navigating it all by yourself any day.**

To quote my best friend, "Your feelings aren't a burden to those who love you."

Let that truth bomb sink in. Realistically, no one will fully understand what you've been through and what you've experienced. People can empathize, but no one truly knows and comprehends your entire story. No one is inside your head, thinking what you think and feeling what you feel, but that doesn't really matter. A big part of healing is allowing people into your world and sharing your truth with them. People don't need to fully understand your experience to hold you up when you feel like falling to pieces.

It's time for you to make the effort to let people in. Make sure you say yes to nights out with friends and that you show up for family get-togethers. If a friend calls to meet up, get out of bed, put on some clothes, and go meet them (even if it's the last thing you want to do). If your friends don't take the initiative to get together, then make it your goal to plan something. It will distract your mind and give you something to look forward to.

If you don't have a solid support system, take comfort knowing that, at the very least, you have me (don't be shy to reach out to me!)—another person in this world who has suffered from episodes of crippling loneliness. I know this offering doesn't lessen your suffering or ease that dull ache you've been carrying with you, but suffering appreciates company. I hope there's comfort for you knowing that

I'm here, a fellow soul who has been through a divorce and has been victimized by loneliness. I also hope you can take comfort knowing that I was able to move past loneliness and heal in a beautiful way.

I learned how to fill up my life so that the void created by my divorce disappeared. You can do the same. I know you can.

LONELINESS IS A FEELING, NOT A FACT

A wise person once told me that *thoughts become things.* Our personal narratives are shaped by the thoughts we tell ourselves and the feelings that course through our hearts. In no way do I ever want to discount anyone's feelings because feelings are very real. They can hit us fucking hard, make an impact on our behaviors, alter our lives, and make it unbearable to keep living. If feelings infiltrate our minute-to-minute thinking, it's very easy for them to become the only reality we see.

And our feelings sometimes become so real to us that they become facts in our lives.

During the early stages of my separation, I didn't have the self-awareness to tell myself that I could move through feelings of loneliness. I didn't have the motivation to do things to help myself move through these feelings. I just stayed stuck and allowed my loneliness to become a very real fact that overtook me, which effectively halted my healing.

I had to wake up to the fact that I was allowing myself to suffer greatly because of a feeling. I also had to remind myself that I could shift this feeling.

Even though your loneliness might be horrible and make you feel awful, every minute of every day, I want to reiterate that your loneliness is a feeling and NOT a fact.

Know that you have the power to change your feelings and completely overcome any loneliness haunting you right now. The first step to overcoming is to face the feeling. I know this advice might be easier said than done. It can be terrifying to admit that we're in pain. Fears of being judged block us from being real. As a coping mechanism, we suppress.

Right now, you must be stronger than any fear that may be getting in the way of your healing. It's really important that you do the opposite of any impulse you have to push down your loneliness so it becomes invisible to anyone but you.

If you want to overcome the pain of loneliness, you can't suppress it.

The best thing I did was admit to myself that I was lonely. I allowed my loneliness to wash over me. I lived in the feeling and embraced what was happening in my mind and heart.

I cried.

I screamed.

I felt every feel.

I didn't limit anything.

I allowed myself to break down.

I let it all out.

Every feeling that came up was valid, and I allowed myself to experience each one.

Something that helped me was expressing my feelings in my journal. I would write the phrase *I feel lonely because* . . . and would follow it with every single reason why I was feeling lonely. Some days, I would write one sentence, while other days, I'd fill pages and pages. I let everything come out in my writing. Journaling allowed my feelings to be free, especially those that I had kept locked up for so long.

Something interesting happened during this practice. I unintentionally flipped the script. I started to embrace the opportunity of loneliness instead of focusing on the negatives.

It started one day when I wrote, *I feel lonely because I have no one to watch TV with*. In that moment, the feeling was very real to me; however, an interesting thing happened as I added more reasons to the list. At the end of my journaling session that day, I looked back on what I had written. When I reread my statement, I started to work through how great it was to not have to cater to anyone else when I watched TV. I started to look at the positives of watching TV alone: I could watch whatever I wanted for however long I wanted. I could hog the remote. I could watch every rom-com my heart desired.

The loneliness I had been feeling, that had felt like a prison, had suddenly transformed into a vehicle for freedom, independence, self-awareness, and personal discovery.

In that moment, I realized that **being alone didn't have to equal being lonely.**

These two experiences could be entirely different. If you allow yourself to feel loneliness and live through your feelings, you can authentically start to shift the narrative in your mind. Instead of sitting in loneliness, sit in the potential that being alone offers. Shift your mindset to see loneliness not as a horrible experience but rather as an opportunity to get to know yourself again.

Solitude provides you with the space to rediscover exactly who you are and how you want your life to look.

It is better to find joy and self-love in being alone than spending a lifetime of loneliness being in a broken marriage or being surrounded by people who make you feel small or don't value or appreciate you for who you are.

Being alone gets rid of any noise or distraction that was getting in the way of you being your best, most authentic self. Being alone and unattached allows you the space to do what you want, go where you want, live where you want, travel where you want, work where you want, and spend time with whomever you want. You don't have to check with anyone before you do anything. You don't have to ask permission about a single thing.

If you're able to shift your mindset away from the pain of loneliness into a place of embracing the opportunity of being alone, you'll realize that you've been given a phenomenal gift from the universe: the gift of rediscovering exactly who you are!

PRACTICES THAT HELP OVERCOME LONELINESS

Even if you're doing your best to shift your mindset to a place of embracing being alone instead of suffering under loneliness, it can sometimes be extremely difficult. Just like any shift in thinking, it can sometimes take very deliberate practices to shift your thoughts.

Here is a list of some of the actions that helped me when I was feeling gutted by loneliness:

Picking Up a New Hobby

You may have a lot of free time these days, which might be part of the reason you feel so lonely. Figuring out what to do with all that extra time is a big part of the divorce process.

One action that really helped me was picking up a new hobby. For me, it was writing and blogging. For you, it could be anything! Maybe you start painting, take up photography, join a competitive sports team, take a yoga class, join a bowling league, start a weekly basketball game with friends, join a book club, take up swimming, or start scrapbooking.

If you are sitting idle, the dark thoughts are more likely to haunt you. Picking up a new hobby is an excellent way to distract yourself to avoid going down the *loneliness rabbit hole*. A new hobby will not only distract your mind but will also give you a new sense of purpose. Something new could provide structure and purpose to your week or help fan the self-esteem fires. If you find something that you love (that you're also somewhat skilled at), just watch as you start to feel better about yourself overall. After every single writing session, I feel proud of what I've created and great about myself, overall.

One of the most important outcomes of a new hobby is the like-lihood that it will lead to new friendships and relationships. My blog has led to friendships with people from around the world. I've connected with thousands of people who have lived through a similar experience and who are passionate about the same issues.

Your hobby may not lead to a network of people around the world; however, at the very least, it's likely to lead to new friendships with people who have the same passion as you. If you enroll in that paint-ing class, there'll be chances every week to get to know new people.

If you join a bowling league, watch as your social circle suddenly widens. If you start a photography Instagram account, there's the potential to connect with others who have the same passion. These new relationships can end up being just what you need to help diminish some of the loneliness you are feeling.

Helping Is Healing

During my divorce, I became friends with a woman who was going through a divorce after thirty-five years of marriage. We helped each other along the road to healing. She taught me that the best way to serve yourself is to serve others.

She explained to me that early in her divorce, she was extremely lost and very lonely. A friend suggested that she spend some time volunteering. She liked the idea and decided to volunteer once a week at a local homeless shelter. It was the one thing outside of work that got her out of the house. Over the weeks, she found that she not only enjoyed volunteering but looked forward to it. Eventually, volunteering at that homeless shelter became the highlight of her week.

Volunteering filled her up with so much light. She was able to put aside her pain for a few hours a week and focus on the betterment of others. The people she helped made an impact on her heart in a profound way. She found herself filled with purpose, hope, and joy.

The last while, you've probably been so focused on your pain that there's likely been little emotional space for the service of others.

Volunteering shifts your internal focus off you to thinking about others. This shift is perhaps just what you need to fill your heart with light. Volunteering may help you find purpose in knowing that you are doing service for others in need. You might uncover new passions, discover things about yourself, form new friendships, create new bonds, and make new connections in the community.

Get Active

As many of us already know, exercise releases endorphins that elevate mood. Being active can help you feel happier. And being happier helps ease the sting of loneliness.

When I'm feeling particularly alone, I take my workout public and get active around other people. I go to the gym, take a workout class, or practice yoga. These activities help get my mind off things and force me to be around other people. Thus, I feel a little less lonely.

If you've never worked out before, getting active can be intimidating and feel daunting, but there's no time like the present. And, in all honesty, it doesn't matter what's happened in the past or what level of fitness you're currently at. The point is that you're choosing to exercise *now*. Once you make the choice to incorporate some fitness into your routine, you've taken the first step toward a healthy habit that will help you with your loneliness.

Take it slow at first. The point isn't necessarily about how much you're working out, if you're going to the gym, or if you're following a routine or any other "rules" you think you should follow. Plain and simple, it's about making that effort to increase physical activity.

Try to commit to moving your body once a week. It could be alone on a jog in nature or in a gym surrounded by others. You could sign up for a workout class and let the instructor lead. Maybe you commit to a yoga class every Friday to de-stress from the week. Maybe you choose to walk once a week around your neighborhood.

It doesn't matter what you do—just get those endorphins flowing. Not only will you start feeling healthier and better about yourself, but you'll also start to feel the impact of those elevated endorphins.

Showing Up for Your Life

It took a long time, but I eventually realized that I could move through loneliness by not allowing it to dictate how I was going to live my life. I knew that it was part of my journey and that I had to make some space for it, but I didn't need to suffer through it alone, in the dark, under the covers.

Even though loneliness was my constant companion, I could still show up for the rest of my life.

Once I realized that, everything changed.

I met my friends for drinks, got away on girls' trips, went shopping, and hit up my favorite yoga class. I traveled, visited with my family, and threw myself into work. Essentially, even while struggling with loneliness, I decided to continue to do all the things I loved.

I realized that life had moved on and I could either move on with it or stay stuck in my feelings alone. I decided to show up and face the world. I decided to be present. I decided to live my life.

Eventually, the loneliness became less and less present. By embracing it, but not allowing it to swallow me whole, I ended up liberating myself from it all.

Gratitude Goes a Long Way

During my divorce, when I was feeling particularly lonely, I decided to start a Gratitude Challenge. Every morning, I challenged myself to write down three things I was thankful for that day. I could write down anything that came into my mind. Some days, I wrote a statement of gratitude for my daily cup of coffee. Other days, I wrote about my friends and family or the freedom I had to be creative in my work. The longer I participated in the challenge, the more I realized that I had so much to be thankful for in my life.

Through the challenge, I realized that I took a lot for granted in my life. My home, bed, food on the table, warm clothes, car, health, family, friends, and so on. This realization put into perspective the advantages and privileges I have in my life and the gifts that have come my way.

I got to the point where I realized that almost everything in my life was a luxury, including . . . my divorce. I know. That's a pretty bold statement, but stick with me.

I realized that there are people in our world who don't have the luxury to access divorce, even in situations of violence and abuse. There are people who are trapped in their marriage and would give anything to have the freedom to divorce, something that put things into perspective for me.

The day I woke up feeling gratitude for my divorce was a big turning point. It was one of the first days when I didn't feel loneliness and heartache. On that day, I wrote all about my appreciation for the opportunity that had unfolded in my life. I sent gratitude into the universe for shifting my path. Tears fell as I wrote thanks for the unknown and the opportunity ahead to pursue everything I've ever wanted for myself.

It was in that moment that I realized that all my loneliness was a tremendous gift from the universe to rediscover exactly who I am and the life I want, all on my own. On this day, I said thank you, over and over, for this second shot at living the life of my dreams.

I haven't stopped saying thank you ever since.

You're Going to Make It.

Your Task

Write a list of the things you can start doing in your own life to help you cope with the loneliness you feel.

- Is there a new hobby you'd like to explore?

- A friend you haven't seen in a while?

- Somewhere you'd like to visit?

- A club you want to take part in?

- A gym or a fitness class you want to join?

- Write out your list and make a plan for yourself.

Grief is heavy.
Don't carry the load
alone.

FIVE

Managing
THE WAVES OF GRIEF

The common understanding of grief is that we go through a series of five stages while grieving. If you do any research on grief, you can easily learn about each stage. A basic list is as follows: denial, anger, bargaining, depression, and finally, acceptance. Based on this understanding, you would think the grief experience happens in a specific order of stages and that each stage has a timeline.

Unfortunately, grief is far more complex than the five prescribed stages.

Following the end of my marriage, I felt all five stages, but not the way one would expect if looking at each stage as a singular experience. My experience with grief was this: each stage felt like one small shard of glass that had broken off an enormous window of grief. Each of these tiny shards that made up that one "grief window" hit me at different times, while also all at the same time. And that window of grief that had created all the shards that were slicing me open was only one small window in an enormous mural of windows that made up a piece of artwork titled *GRIEF*.

I didn't feel each stage of grief as a closed container. Instead, I felt shards of all stages at the same time. They pierced my skin, my soul, and my memories in every waking moment.

The shards of denial sliced me open at the same time as shards of anger, sadness, bargaining, and depression. Not to mention the shards of anxiety, worthlessness, regret, and hopelessness. If I've learned anything from my divorce, it's that grief isn't linear—it's not even day-to-day.

Grief is a second-to-second experience.

One moment, you'll feel 100 percent healed. The next second, your knees will buckle under you as extreme sadness sweeps over. The next minute, you'll feel so enraged that you won't be able to function.

Grieving isn't linear. Not even a tiny bit. It's a huge raging storm that you have no control over. The waves hit you hard at different times and in different places in a haphazard way.

At the same time, we must grieve to heal. It's the only path to rebuilding our lives after trauma and loss.

I spent years waiting for grief to pass. I read self-help books and went to therapy. I engaged in self-care and pursued self-love. I changed my internal dialogue and went out of my way to be more kind to myself. Still, grief crippled me at the most inopportune and inappropriate times. Grief doesn't care what you're doing and doesn't consider your day-to-day responsibilities. Just when you think you're going to have a truly wonderful day, grief can be there to remind you that you aren't fully healed.

I vividly remember having to excuse myself from family functions, crying at my desk at work, canceling plans at the last minute because I couldn't get out of bed, and unexpectedly lashing out at friends. Grief creeps in the shadows, fooling you, convincing you that you've healed, then striking when you least expect it and aren't prepared to cope.

So, how do you manage the overwhelming feelings of grief? How do you continue living your life as normally as possible even though you feel everything except normal? How do you continue living when you feel like you want everything to end? Even though it might seem impossible right now, grief can be managed, you can overcome, and more than that, you can fucking thrive.

ACKNOWLEDGE YOUR PAIN

I didn't confront things for a long time. It was too painful. Instead, I distracted myself with anything that would take my mind off all the horrible things I was thinking every second of the day.

I also drank to forget my pain. Bottle after bottle of wine, in the evenings, when I was alone in the house and no one was watching. Unfortunately, the wine had the opposite effect of what I wanted. Instead of numbing things, like I had hoped, I found myself overly emotional. You can only imagine how well this helped with my healing (newsflash: it didn't). True healing only started when I turned away from the distractions just long enough to finally acknowledge how broken I was.

Even if you willingly chose this path in your life, divorce can be unbelievably painful and traumatic. The loss felt after a divorce is not overly different from the loss felt following a death because divorce is a death of so much in your life. The pain of all the loss can be crippling.

It can take people years to cope with the aftermath of divorce due to the trauma sustained.

I once read a story about a woman who had been married twice and had lost both husbands. The first marriage ended when her husband passed away. The second marriage ended through a divorce. When the woman was asked which experience was more painful, she quickly and easily stated, "Divorce."

She went on to explain that the grief of divorce hit her much harder than losing her first husband. She maintained that there was a certain level of finality to death and that those left behind can eventually find acceptance. She explained that with divorce, acceptance takes much longer and there are a lot of regrets.

Of course, this opinion is just one person's, and there are many factors that could have made an impact on it. As well, her relationship with each of these men would have been different; however, if anyone could measure the pain of divorce compared to the pain of death, she's as good a judge as any because she went through both.

Please don't underplay your pain. It's real. It's raw. It's authentic. Don't let anyone tell you otherwise.

Divorce causes a dramatic change in your life. It's inevitable and unavoidable. You lose so much of your old life—family, possessions, property, traditions, everyday routines, time with your children, a spouse, and your vision of what you thought your life would look like for the rest of your days. It's a lot to confront and process. At any given moment, you could be fighting an internal struggle, dark thoughts, and heartbreak.

Often, we hide from the pain. It can be incredibly hard to face the trauma.

Unfortunately, hiding is, in fact, the opposite of what needs to be done. The longer you put off confronting your grief, the longer it will take to get back on your feet and heal your invisible wounds.

I had to acknowledge my pain. It was important to confront the hard reality that my life was in turmoil and would never be what it once was. I had to confront the fact that I was experiencing excruciating pain. Being honest with myself was such an important step in my healing journey.

CONFIDE IN SOMEONE YOU TRUST

It's easy to isolate yourself when you're grieving. Being alone allows you to feel every emotion without fear of judgment. You can cry all night, attack your journal with words of hatred, and rip up pictures with vigor. There is something extremely therapeutic about processing grief all alone.

At the same time, isolated coping for an extended period can become harmful and damaging because you can stay trapped there. If no one is keeping tabs on your grieving, you may never emerge from your suffering. Confiding in someone you trust releases your thoughts and emotions to another human who can help lighten the load that rests on your heart. The people you confide in can help comfort you and be there to check on you to ensure you aren't self-destructing.

When I finally decided to reveal my suffering to someone, I initially confided in my sister, my therapist, and a couple of my close friends, which helped me unload some of what was going on inside my mind onto trusted people in my life, all of whom had room in their hearts to take on some of my pain. These people also had great advice, offered empathy, and helped me feel not so alone in my pain.

GRIEF CAN TRIGGER COMPLEX AND UNEXPECTED EMOTIONS

If grief were simple, you wouldn't be reading this chapter. It's complicated, difficult to manage, and unbelievably unique to each person who goes through the experience.

When I was dealing with my grief, I had feelings of anger I had never felt before. The feelings were extremely raw, and unfortunately affected my actions. I had yelling outbursts at people I loved. I punched pillows. I screamed in my car. I drew circle after circle in my journal with so much force that I tore the book apart. I imagined my ex-husband being with me, and I yelled every single angry thought I had at the imaginary figure. I was surprised and taken aback by my angry outbursts, as I had never before in my life identified, or been referred to by others, as an angry person. Even so, there I was, a ball of rage.

I went through episodes of anxiety when I spiraled into a mess of thoughts of constant worry and fixation. I suffered close to a year of situational depression that led me to the darkest place I had ever been. Anxiety and depression were mental health struggles that were completely foreign to me before my divorce. It was difficult for me to admit to myself that I was suffering and that I needed targeted intervention and help to heal.

Like I said: unexpected and complex emotions.

If your grief triggers unexpected emotions and behaviors, know that it is normal and part of the process. Honor your emotions by allowing yourself to feel each one. It is only when we fully feel each emotion that we allow our minds to process them—it is the only way we can start to move through anything and heal.

YOUR GRIEF WILL BE A UNIQUE EXPERIENCE THAT NO ONE ELSE WILL FULLY COMPREHEND

Everyone's ability (or possibly their inability) to cope with heartbreak is different. Some people can navigate through divorce easily and can move forward into the next chapter in their lives with little strife. At the same time, divorce can bring some to their breaking point. I was crippled by my divorce, emotionally and mentally. I couldn't cope with all the loss I felt, and I had an extremely difficult time adjusting to my different path. It took me a very long time to fully heal and arguably much longer than people in my life expected. However, it was part of my journey.

The fact that it took me so long to grieve doesn't make my experience with grief any more authentic than someone who is able to move on quickly. The length of time it takes to grieve does not validate one person over the other. The grief process is unique to each person who is suffering and will be different for everyone. This fact is true even if you know someone who has lived through loss and grief. This fact is true even if you know someone who is going through it right now. This fact is true even if someone is experiencing grief because of the same situation as you (in our case, divorce). No matter the length of time, each person's experience is real, raw, and soul changing.

If other people in your life try to understand your grief but don't seem to get it, be patient with them. They are doing their best to be supportive. No one can fully understand your complex set of emotions. Do your best to communicate what you're feeling, and hopefully, the people in your life will be the loving listeners you need in that moment.

COPING WITH MEMORIES

When you are coping with divorce, you can have days, weeks, months, or even years when you feel like you're healed only to suddenly find yourself missing the one person you never thought you'd miss again. Your mind will trick you because it so desperately wants to be healed and happy again; however, the difficult reality is that there is still an unhealed wound lying deep inside you.

Memories continued to haunt my mind for a long time, even when I thought I was completely healed.

I would be going about my day, thinking I was healed, and then suddenly, a memory would float into my brain that would take out my figurative knees. The memories would range. Some of them brought a smile to my face. Others I wished I could forget. The shadows continued to haunt my mind, and I would cripple under the weight of my past. These memories would remind me of what I had lost and the reality of my life: I was experiencing divorce and had to start over when that was the last thing I ever wanted for my life. I would exist there, in that headspace, reliving the past for hours or days on end.

The strangest thing was that even though I wanted a divorce and was sure of my decision, there were times when I missed my marriage and my ex more than I could stand.

Maybe you're like me—not wanting to be married anymore but still missing your former spouse. Maybe you miss your Saturday morning ritual or hanging out on the couch watching your favorite show together. Maybe you miss holidays with your in-laws or just the day-to-day traditions you had established as a couple.

Maybe you miss a lot of things.

My advice is to not fight or resist your memories. Let them come and embrace them. Be authentic to what your body is feeling and what your mind is thinking. Relive the joy. Cry for the pain. Embrace every single thing. There's no point fighting anything. If you deny yourself these memories, you'll deny yourself the grief you must suffer to move forward. If you deny these memories, you'll deny yourself the emotions that you need to feel to eventually be okay.

If someone asks if you're all right, be genuine and tell them about what you're experiencing. Your community of friends and family will rally and shower you with kindness. Those who love you will support you. Let them hold you up when you feel like falling to pieces.

With time, the memories will fade.

SEEK OUT SUPPORT FROM PEOPLE WHO CARE ABOUT YOU

While grieving, I didn't want any of my friends or family to truly know what I was going through. In the best of times, I don't like to appear weak or vulnerable. During one of the hardest times in my life, I especially didn't want my friends or family to know what I was experiencing. While grieving my divorce, I was fighting a painful internal battle, and I didn't want anyone to witness my suffering. I didn't know if anyone would understand, and I didn't know how to properly communicate what I was feeling. So, I hid.

I believed that my suffering was a burden to others. I believed that everyone was better off not knowing what was going on in my mind. I thought it was better to just be alone and get through it on my own. I shut people out. I stopped returning calls and didn't bother to respond to texts. It took too much energy. I spent nights alone in tears. I was living through an extremely unhealthy time in my life.

What I eventually learned was that isolation did not lead to healing.

Finally opening up to others was an important step that ended up being my saving grace. My family and friends lifted my spirits and reminded me of all the beauty and joy that was in my life. They made me laugh and listened when I cried. Even if it was short-lived and only in the moment, family and friends helped me feel happier.

I always felt lighter after a visit with a loved one.

During your grieving process, even if you want to shut everyone out, do your best to keep loved ones close. One of the best things you can do is call or text a friend or family member every single day, even if it's just one person and it's a quick conversation. It's really important that you make the effort. It will help remind you that you aren't alone and there are people who care about you.

SUPPORT YOURSELF EMOTIONALLY BY TAKING CARE OF YOURSELF PHYSICALLY

When I initially split from my ex, I lost a ton of weight and was dangerously skinny. At the time, I had no idea how unhealthy I was.

Various people told me that I looked thin and asked if I had lost weight. In my cloud of depression, I interpreted these comments and questions as compliments. They weren't. People were noticing the changes in my body and were concerned. When I finally realized how unhealthy I was, it didn't matter because I was knee-deep in depression.

It took about a year and a half for me to finally take a hard look at myself physically. I was drinking too much. My diet was consistently unhealthy. I wasn't active at all. Changes had to happen.

I cleaned up my diet, cut back on the wine, made it a priority to get enough sleep, and started to jog outside. When I started to make my physical health a priority, I noticed dramatic changes in my mental health and emotional well-being. I felt better and had more energy. My damaged self-confidence and self-worth improved dramatically. I started to appreciate myself again, as a whole person, truly embracing the mind-body connection. I also started to think more positively and feel hope for my future. The connection between physical and mental health was undeniable after I saw the changes that occurred in myself.

KEEP UP YOUR ROUTINE

During the initial days that followed my separation and divorce, I didn't have much motivation or energy. I existed in my bed most days.

Daily tasks seemed daunting. I had felt hopeless for so long that it seemed almost impossible that anything would help; however, getting back into a routine helped me regain my sense of purpose again and was exactly the thing I needed. I started to feel like myself again. I was reminded of the person I was before grief took over my life.

You may also go through a period of not wanting to get out of bed, but hear these words: It is really important to keep up a routine. It will help distract your mind, keep you busy, and help you maintain a sense of order and purpose in your life when everything feels so chaotic. Even simple things like doing housework and taking a shower can help you have small moments in your day when you feel better. These small moments can add up quite a bit.

TRUST IN YOUR JOURNEY

I've read inspirational quotes, but it wasn't until I lived through grief that I truly understood how true those quotes are.

Grief isn't linear, a truth we know and realize. It comes in waves, and sometimes, the worst episodes will hit like tsunamis. One moment you may feel fully healed, only to find yourself suddenly on the floor, unable to move. My grieving process was all over the place and episodes of anger and sorrow hit when I thought I was over everything.

If you're in a downswing, don't lose hope. It is completely normal and part of the process. If you bury your emotions and don't fully experience them now, they'll haunt you in the future when you least expect it. You have to ride the waves that suck you deep into the darkness. You have to feel every horrible shard of pain and agony and let the tears fall. It's more than likely that you'll feel hopeless and (unfortunately) worthless at different times during this process; however, you must move through your pain if you have any desire to authentically heal. You have to go through the downswing to get back up to a place of happiness, peace, and acceptance. Think of it like surfing through the ocean waves. Some knock you right down, while you can coast and surf smoothly on others. But if you were to hide away from it all, you wouldn't get to experience the sheer high you receive from surfing the ocean tide or feel the cool, salty water on your skin or the rays of sunshine that hit you in the face while you await another wave.

No matter what you're feeling and how much grief you're suffering, trust that you are exactly where you need to be at this moment in your life. Through your suffering and eventual healing, you will learn some of the most important lessons of your life. If you embrace your pain, when the grief storm settles, you'll emerge much stronger and ready to take on the next chapter of your journey.

I'll end this chapter with something I wrote during my healing journey:

You broke me into a million pieces that laid scattered for a very long time. Each fragment was a painful reminder of my trauma, loss, grief, and heartbreak.

It took a lot of work and a long time to heal, but I finally got to a place of peace and acceptance.

Now, I'm a beautiful patchwork of lessons from my past, gratitude for my present, and hope for my future.

You're Going to Make It.

Your Task

Write a list of things you can do to help you get through your grief.

- Should you join a gym?
- Spend more time in nature?
- Call up a friend?
- Journal?
- Allow yourself to break down?

What are the things you can do right now to help facilitate the grief process and help you heal?

The bravest thing
you can ever do is
survive when all you
want to do is give up.

SIX

My Descent
INTO DEPRESSION

The end of a marriage can be sudden and unexpected. Any expectation you had about your future is uprooted. The dream of lifelong commitment is destroyed. Ideas about what your life would look like are smashed into pieces. And for many of us, it can feel like we are veering away from tradition, culture, and societal norms. Divorce changes everything, and the whole process can seem impossible to navigate. Unfortunately, you're the only one who can pick up those pieces, step into the unknown, and create a new life on your own.

In case there's any doubt lingering, know this truth: Divorce is horrible for mental health.

Divorce is traumatic. Even though trauma is commonly understood to be caused by an event or experience that is perceived as a life-threatening one, like war, there are psychologists who are shifting our understanding of trauma to be something that can be caused when our perception about what our life will be is destroyed. Divorce is traumatic because it completely shatters lives and threatens our deeply held expectations for our future.

For some people, divorce is the most traumatic experience they will ever go through.

It is no surprise that some divorcées suffer from painful mental health complications following a split. And it's not just trauma but also post-traumatic stress disorder, depression, anxiety, loneliness, stress, and shame. In fact, there is evidence that those who are divorced and separated have a much higher rate of suicide than their married counterparts.[1]

Everyone's stories and experiences are different. Some people are excellent at coping with divorce and the transition that follows. However, others have experiences like mine. Divorce rocked me to the core and almost destroyed me.

Before my divorce, I was very happy, an eternal optimist, and positive to a fault. I always saw the bright side and expected the best. Struggles came my way, and I brushed them off because I believed that every hardship was manageable. My self-esteem was unbelievably high, and I could cope with anything. I also was emotionally stable.

My favorite saying back then, which I shared with anyone who would listen, was "Everything works out—maybe differently than you expect, but it always works out."

This belief remained true until I experienced the earth-shattering, heartbreaking reality that was my divorce. At the end of everything, I had lost my marriage, my husband, my house, possessions, more than all my money, friends, family, and any idea of what my future held for me. I also believed that I had lost my chance to have children. We separated when I was thirty, and we didn't have kids. I didn't know if I'd have the opportunity in the future with someone else. Consequently, I had to face the real possibility of a childless future, and I wanted children.

While facing all this loss, I was also dealing with some other incredible stressors in my life. Everything combined pushed me past my ability to adapt and cope. Somewhere between married and suddenly single, I found myself falling deeper and deeper into depression.

There were many days I couldn't get out of bed. I had crying fits at work when no one was watching. I felt weak to the point that I'd have to lie down. I lost a tremendous amount of weight and looked as *skeletal* as I ever had. I felt hopeless and believed myself to be worthless.

The most heartbreaking fact was that I saw no way out.

Even though there's a whole mental health campaign structured around the idea that *it gets better*, I saw no *better* in sight and didn't think it would ever get better for me. The darkness consumed my mind, and I believed that I was destined to live in that place. I saw no light and wanted everything to end. At the time, I thought life couldn't get any better and that everyone would be better off if I were gone.

I had depression, and on most days, it swallowed me whole.

I was in so much pain and felt so alone. I couldn't live with the pain, nor could I cope with the memories I desperately wanted to forget. I also thought I had become a burden to my friends and family and was convinced they would be better off without me and my *complaining*. I felt so pathetic and wanted to do everyone a *favor*. In my mind, that favor was disappearing forever.

I remember writing in my journal, "I just want to melt into the ground and be gone forever. Everyone will be better off."

No one in my life knew, but I was silently fighting for my life. During the darkest point of my depression, suicidal ideation took over my mind. I had a plan for how I'd end my life. I came up with it one night when I couldn't handle the pain any longer. *I'd end my life with pills*, I had silently decided.

Every time I got the urge to end my life, I'd sit on the floor of my bedroom and would empty pill bottles, thinking about how easy it would be to be free. I would visualize myself swallowing them all, quietly drifting away and finally being free of the pain. I would sit there for hours, contemplating the option I had created for myself. There was an odd comfort knowing that I had the power to end my pain at any time. At least I had this control when I felt so out of control of so many things in my life. I couldn't bear my life. I felt so alone, and the grief was crippling. On those incredibly dark nights, I had to convince myself not to do what I thought was the only thing that would end my pain. This dance went on for months.

I coped by isolating myself. Hiding my pain seemed easier than confronting anything. On those lonely nights, I drank to numb the pain. One glass of wine turned into a bottle. One bottle turned into more bottles.

I was ashamed I was going through a divorce at a relatively young age. I was ashamed to be starting over with what I believed to be nothing. I was ashamed that I thought about ending my life. I was ashamed that I was drinking alone. I was ashamed that I had depression.

Shame engulfed me.

I knew things were bad when suicide became a daily consideration. Regularly, I thought about ending it all. I thought it was the only action that would stop my pain. Thankfully, I never did anything to harm myself. At the same time, I can honestly say that if I still suffered that much emotional pain today, I would no longer be here.

Mental illness has strange effects on a logical and stable mind. Before I experienced divorce, I was the person who could cope with any situation. While coping with the loss that resulted from my divorce, I found myself unable to cope with even small disappointments.

I look at my ability to cope as a battery. The woman I was before my divorce was still living inside, but unfortunately, I had been drained. Every traumatic event that I experienced was a huge drain on my battery. The immense loss of so many things in my life at the same time continued to cause a drain. It all built up, and it wasn't long before I found myself running on empty, and when that happened, it became almost impossible to charge.

I also found it extremely difficult to come to terms with, and truly accept, what was happening. I was too proud to admit there was something wrong going on in my brain. I was embarrassed enough that I was going through a divorce, and I didn't want to also admit that I needed help. At the same time, the only way I was going to get better was to admit to myself and others what was going on.

After much suffering and many dark days, I started to inch toward an admission that I had a problem and needed help.

I was finally able to be honest with both myself and others about my struggles when I realized that health is health: mental, physical, or otherwise. Similar to how a broken leg hinders your ability to function at full capacity, my mental health was affecting my ability to function and cope. I also started to think that healing was possible and there was a chance I could overcome my struggle.

FIRST STEP: THERAPY AND CONFRONTING SHAME

After a lot of self-destructive behavior, emotional outbursts, days spent depressed in bed, anxiety episodes, and trauma triggers, I finally got to a point where I knew I needed professional help. My well-being depended on it.

Therapy was my saving grace. It was pivotal to my healing. However, before I could fully tackle my depression with my therapist, I had to deal with the shame I felt. I had to identify what about this experience was making me feel so much shame. I had to be blunt and honest with that voice inside my head, embrace my extreme emotions, and confront my damaging thoughts (even those dark suicidal ones). I couldn't hide from the truth any longer. Hiding had not served me and had just contributed to my suffering.

I give anyone coping with shame this same advice: *If you run from your pain, you'll never overcome it.* Shame grows exponentially in places of isolation. If you hide from it, shame will take over every moment of your day. The first step to overcoming is acknowledging there's a problem. Once you admit to yourself what you're feeling, you can take the next steps. For me, the next step was booking that first therapy appointment.

Even on the days when I could barely get out of bed, I got myself to therapy. After every session, I felt like I was inching my way back to a healthy mind. During therapy sessions, any dark thoughts inside my mind were released to a caring professional who listened and helped guide me to acceptance and healing. Therapy helped validate these thoughts and feelings, while also showing me ways to cope and eventually move forward. My therapist helped me work through shame, as well as the loss and trauma that was at the root of my depression. I cannot emphasize enough how much therapy has truly made an impact on my life. It's an amazing gift I gave myself, and continue to give myself, when needed.

If you are struggling, please be kind to yourself. There are a lot of divorcées feeling the same way, right now, as you read these words. You are in good company!

Remind yourself every day that it's okay to not be okay.

You don't have to be bright and cheery. You don't have to please others with a smile. Love yourself enough to feel every feel, even the sad and dark ones. And while you are on the self-love journey, book a therapy appointment.

JOURNALING

During my divorce, journaling helped me tremendously. There were many days I was a prisoner in my mind because I had about a million heavy thoughts and feelings weighing me down, making it almost impossible to function.

Writing became a release.

I filled the pages of my journal with all my thoughts and feelings, no matter how dark. Some entries were a bit dull, while others were filled with passion, rage, and sorrow. It didn't matter what I wrote, it was more about the act of getting my thoughts and feelings out of my mind. I didn't have to hang onto them because I had an outlet to get them out.

On the days I journaled, I always felt lighter. The mere act of putting my thoughts and feelings to paper helped me release some of the loneliness I was feeling on the many nights that I had to keep myself company on the couch and go to bed alone. Did journaling make me feel totally healed? No. But every time I wrote, I always felt better, even by a little bit. That was enough for me at that moment.

Don't worry if you don't have a fancy journal to write in. You can journal in a scribbler, on your phone, on your computer, or on napkins. The point isn't the tool you use, it's the act of getting your emotions out. There is something cathartic about expressing all your emotions on paper.

If you can fit journaling in every day, that's amazing! I would suggest carving out a certain time each day that works for you, as it will help you form a habit. The best time may be in the evening after you've lived through another day wrought with heavy feelings. Or maybe you want to write first thing after you wake up. Writing at the same time each day can help you stay on track. With that said, you don't have to journal every day. You may choose to write every other day, once a week, or just when you feel the need. There are no rules or right ways to do it. Personally, I only journaled when I felt the need. That was enough and helped me.

I still reread some entries. I like to reflect on how much I've grown since the start of the divorce process. It is sometimes therapeutic to remind myself of the dark places my mind went to after the end of my marriage in order to appreciate how much I have to be thankful for in my life now.

At the same time, there are a lot of entries I've never read again. Journaling isn't about having a record of your thoughts to go back to. There are many people who fill journals, only to throw them out at the end. Journaling is mainly about the act of release. For many people, once they've released, they can move on.

CONNECTING WITH OTHERS WHO'VE LIVED THROUGH THE SAME EXPERIENCE

You'll be surprised how fast self-acceptance grows once you start cultivating relationships with others who have lived your experience and can empathize with your plight. Joining together with others who share your experience and talking about what's going on in your life is incredibly therapeutic! Being part of a community of like-minded people who'll lift you up when you feel like you're going to fall apart is definitely healing!

When I was initially separated, hardly anyone in my life was part of the *divorce club*. I desperately needed to connect with others who had lived through or were currently living through a divorce. I didn't know where to look in my own life, so I turned to the internet.

Even though it may sound fickle, social media helped me. On Boxing Day in the first year I was single, I started an Instagram account where I posted exactly what I was feeling about my divorce. At that time, the account was anonymous. I didn't post my photo or name to anything. I made this choice so that I didn't feel the need to censor myself. This account became an online journal where I revealed my thoughts and emotions in a real and raw way.

People started liking, commenting, and following. I quickly realized there were other divorce warriors out there who were just like me. I started to connect with so many people who had lived through or were living through a divorce. For someone who had felt so alone and isolated, I had suddenly found my community.

We lifted each other up, laughed together, and shared our successes, and we were there for each other when life seemed like it was falling apart. This community understood, better than anyone, what I was going through. They were able to empathize in a way that others couldn't. The support I received from these people was honestly lifesaving. We were living in different countries and weren't physically together as a community, but our connection was real and incredibly therapeutic.

Building relationships with other divorcées did two things. First, I was finally connecting with people when I had been living in a headspace of loneliness and isolation. Second, my feelings were validated by others who were drowning in their own grief following their own divorce. I realized that grief was normal after divorce and that it was okay that I was experiencing what I was feeling.

It was finally okay to not be okay.

The internet isn't the only way to connect. There are so many other routes. Perhaps you'd rather join a talk therapy group or a community program. Maybe it's time to chat with that long-lost cousin who recently split from her husband or to reach out to colleagues who've been through a separation. Simply stated, find an avenue where you can connect with people going through a divorce. It'll make you feel less alone and help you start tackling all the complicated emotions you are experiencing.

OPENING UP TO TRUSTED FAMILY AND FRIENDS

Taking away the veil of secrecy and opening up to other divorcées gave me the courage to be honest about my struggles with my family and friends. Once I did, the people in my life met me with love and support, opening their arms and their hearts, which was exactly what I needed. Did I tell everyone all at once? Definitely not! I started by talking to a couple of trusted individuals, which gave me the courage to be honest with others.

Once I started to be real about what I was going through, it felt like breathing out when I had been holding in for so long. I finally exhaled everything trapped inside.

Please remember that your feelings aren't a burden to the people who care about you. Find someone to confide in who you feel comfortable talking to and who you believe will understand and empathize with your experience. Sharing your suffering will help you heal and finally release everything you've been holding in for so long.

SPENDING TIME IN NATURE

Did you know that there's a natural antidepressant waiting just outside your front door? I've been saying it for years: Exposure to nature is a must if you want to improve your mental health. Studies show impressive findings that nature is a strong antidepressant.[2] Spending just twenty to thirty minutes a day outside has proved to relieve anxiety, stress, ADHD, and depression. Time outside increases your energy and improves focus. Nature can also help with the grief process because it leads to improved coping skills, self-awareness, and an elevated mood.

Nature also has incredible healing effects and restorative properties. Some of my most effective healing occurred when I spent time outside.

During the initial stages of my separation, I started to go for runs in the ravine near my home. I wanted to get in shape, and I didn't have money to join a gym or hire a trainer. Exercising outside was a free option. So, I started running.

An interesting occurrence happened on these runs that had nothing to do with exercise. Even if I didn't need a break, I often found myself stopping at the river, taking off my shoes, burying my toes in the grass, breathing in the fresh air, looking at the water flowing past, and basking under the sun. What I didn't know at the time was that these breaks were meeting a desperate need I had for a connection with nature. It was on these breaks that I was reminded of how truly connected everything and everyone is, past, present, and future. I realized that I'm never truly alone, as there's a beautiful world to keep me company alongside all the amazing people that walk its surface.

More than once, on these runs outside, I remember breaking down and sobbing. All the pent-up grief that was lying dormant and frozen deep within my mind was finally freed. It felt like I could finally let go of whatever repressed emotion I was burying.

My initial desire to get in shape quickly grew into a compulsion to run outside every day. On days I didn't run, I felt *out of sorts*, so I ran every day. It became something I craved, something I needed.

Eventually, I realized that my need for these runs outside wasn't actually to get in shape. Instead, my mind was yearning to tap into the incredible healing powers held in nature. It was here that emotional pathways opened up. Nature became one of my biggest healers in helping me repair the darkness that lingered in my mind, spirit, and heart.

If you are suffering, get outside and take in the incredible power that nature holds.

THE ISSUES ARE IN THE TISSUES

During my divorce, I did A LOT of reading; specifically, books about divorce, starting over, rebuilding, coping with grief, and breaking through to the side of happiness. A lot of these books ended up being guides for my transformation.

Through my reading, I discovered the extraordinary degree to which our body holds stress, pain, grief, and trauma. As Gabor Maté beautifully explains in his book *When the Body Says No: The Cost of Hidden Stress*, if you have been through a stressful or traumatic experience, your body could be holding the experience in physical form. Maté explains that if you never address the stress or heal from the trauma, your body could respond, somewhere in your life, with sickness or even worse, critical illness or disease.

Essentially, the issues are in the tissues.

If there is such a strong connection between poor mental health and sickness and illness, there's an equally strong connection between positive physical health and improved mental health. If you're physically healthy, you're more likely to be mentally healthy, or at the very least, your mental health will get a boost. There are so many reasons why exercise is good for your mental health and should be prioritized. For instance, fitness boosts happy chemicals in the brain, calms the nervous system, reduces anxiety, reduces cognitive decline, sharpens thinking, increases relaxation and sleep, reduces depression, and increases self-esteem.

Right now, it's extremely important to treat your body with love. Your overall health depends on it.

Personally, I found tremendous solace in yoga. One of the core principles of the practice is breathing and being present. Focusing on your breath helps settle the mind. It also gives your mind something else to focus on besides the grief you're suffering. A momentary break from mentally beating yourself up may distract you long enough to allow a positive thought to float in. And if you're suffering, any positivity is a welcome distraction.

Another core principle of yoga is self-love. Yoga doesn't ask you to be anything other than you, and it reminds everyone to appreciate how amazing our bodies and minds truly are. This appreciation cultivates self-acceptance and peace. When you practice yoga, you're not just improving your mental health, you are also showering yourself with love.

Yoga encourages the practice of gratitude as well. During my divorce, when I couldn't think of anything to be thankful for, I would attend a yoga class, focus on my breath, and be reminded that at the very least, I was thankful for the breath in my lungs, which is something that some of us take for granted. This focus brought in gratitude, even if that wasn't my original intention. I always felt happier after a class.

When I wasn't practicing yoga, I was going to the gym. It wasn't always easy. Like everyone, there were days I didn't want to get moving. There were days when the last thing I wanted to do was go to the gym; however, I would drag myself there, mainly because I always walked away from a workout feeling better than when I arrived. So even if it was the last thing in the world I wanted to do, I knew it was good for me, so I forced myself to go. Seeing the changes in my body also helped me feel more confident during a time I didn't feel that great about myself.

A workout might be the last thing you want to do, but your mental health depends on you getting in a good sweat! Give yourself this gift as often as you can.

ACCEPTING MY STORY

During my darkest days, I lost all hope that I would ever become my authentic self and be happy again. The truth is that I resisted embracing my story—all of it. There were many times early on in my divorce when I was extremely short-sighted when reflecting on my experience. I would get lost, thinking about the past and immediate present and didn't bother to think about or consider the future. I didn't imagine the possibilities that existed or hold hope for the beauty that could (and would) enter my life. I just remained stuck feeling shame and grief about a failed marriage.

The turning point for me was when I thought seriously about how many years were ahead and the potential that existed for my future. I had spent so much time being ashamed of my current status in life that I forgot to think about what could be. I had to remind myself that I had many decades ahead of me yet and that so much was possible. Happiness could be mine.

The moment I finally acknowledged the endless possibilities that existed for me was the same moment I decided not to waste any more days feeling shame for a failed relationship. There was no point in feeling shame over an experience that would eventually lead to the greatest awakening and evolution of my life.

I fell in love and married my best friend. It didn't last very long, and we didn't have children. The marriage ended, and I had to say good-bye to a lot in my life. I had to pick myself up off the ground and move forward.

This is my story. It's not conventional, but it's mine.

My divorce has forever shaped who I am and who I will become. This experience has made me stronger and more appreciative of all the wonderful things in my life. It has made me incredibly resilient and has changed my perspective on what I can survive. Divorce has changed who I am in an amazing way.

To anyone suffering right now, know that you're not alone. At the very least, I'm here: another soul who has been rocked by the devastation of mental illness after divorce. I understand how painful it can be and how lonely you can feel. But I want you to know this truth—when you're feeling your lowest, never forget that it can get better.

Healing is possible.

Own your story and be proud of all you've been through and how strong you truly are. Love yourself right now for exactly who you are at this very moment. Accept everything that has happened and trust that it's leading you somewhere amazing!

You're Going to Make It.

Your Task

You know yourself best. If your mental health is struggling, write about it!

- What are you struggling with most?
- What do you think is causing this struggle?
- Who or what in your life is negatively affecting your mental health?
- Now, write down the steps you need to take in your life to help improve your mental health!

The real tragedy would be wasting your pain. Use those tears to fuel your drive to create an extraordinary life.

@thealexandraevamay

SEVEN

Dealing
WITH YOUR BELIEFS AND
THE OPINIONS OF OTHERS

When it comes to divorce, everyone seems to have an opinion. Heck, when it comes to every single thing, most people will have an opinion. However, opinions are formed because certain ideals have been drilled into our minds our whole lives. Often, it isn't done purposefully, it's rather an unintentional consequence stemming from our upbringing and from what we see in the world around us.

Your ideas about marriage and divorce were possibly shaped by what you witnessed throughout your childhood. If you were raised by two parents married to each other, and your childhood was relatively happy with parents who seemed to be happy in their marriage, the ideology that marriage is good has probably been unintentionally planted in your mind. This thinking may have grown even stronger if your parents told you outright how important marriage is. Maybe you saw healthy marriages in the parents of your friends. Maybe you witnessed happily married couples on television, in movies, and in the media.

> *This idea that marriage is good isn't just something in your mind, it's an ever-present narrative in our world.*

Just as strong is the complimentary ideology that *divorce is bad*, which holds as much space in popular thought. Divorce isn't something that's often shown in a positive light. In the media, it's usually depicted as a tragedy. We don't have to look much farther than any news story about a celebrity marriage splitting up. Usually, there's a salacious, unsavory, or tragic spin put on the separation. It's hardly ever celebrated as a good move for the couple, or the individuals involved.

Of course, the thinking that *divorce is bad* isn't held by absolutely everyone. Maybe you're one of the lucky few who was raised by an enlightened parent who let you know that both marriage and divorce can be equally positive. Maybe they showed you that divorce can be a magical beginning of a beautiful life. Maybe your support system includes a lot of divorcées who rave about their divorce. Maybe you've seen *Eat Pray Love* too many times to count, and you ascribe to the thinking that happiness is the priority.

Even if you know in your heart that your divorce is a fantastic move for your life, unfortunately, there are still a lot of people who don't ascribe to this way of thinking. Honestly, they can't really be blamed for their world view. The narrative that marriage is good and divorce is bad has been shoved into their minds in the same manner that it was possibly shoved into yours by family, friends, the media, and the world in general. Unfortunately, a lot of the people who live in the *marriage is best* camp will make sure you hear all about it when you're going through your divorce.

Opinions are bound to fly your way. Many of them unwelcome.

During my divorce, I quickly realized that everyone seemed to be an "expert" on marriage and had an opinion to offer.

I compare it to the strange phenomenon that surrounds teaching and schooling. Everyone attended school as a student. Thus, everyone has an opinion about what it is like to be a teacher and how things should happen in a classroom (even though many people have never spent one minute in front of a class). Being a student in a class gives 0 percent insight into what it's like to work as a teacher, but still, many people have opinions about what they think it's like to teach.

Some opinions are accurate, while others are downright insulting. However, there are a lot of people out there who like to feverishly communicate what they believe, even if the opinion is unfounded, uneducated, or completely misses the mark. This same theory applies to opinions about marriage and divorce.

Many adults are in marriages of their own, have been in a relationship at some point in their adult lives, or witnessed the marriage of their parents. This relative experience that everyone has with relationships leads to a mountain of opinions from people in your life about your marriage or . . . your divorce.

Unfortunately, some opinions will hurt. Those are the ones to watch out for.

Some opinions will get at insecurities sitting idle in your brain. Some will touch on things you're thinking far too often to admit. Some will make you question the direction of your life. Some will make you feel sad, angry, or worried. Some will make you doubt your decisions. Some will make you feel worthless. Some will make you feel alone.

At the same time, the opinions of others won't be all bad. Some opinions and advice will help. Some will make you reflect and help you grow. The best opinions will help shape your journey and will lead you to personal evolution. The key is listening to the opinions you deem valuable and tuning out the advice that doesn't serve you.

What worked for me was to remember that most people are just trying to help. They aren't purposefully being malicious or unkind. They are doing what they think is best. They are sharing their opinions because they think it will help you. Unfortunately, delivery is everything, and sometimes the delivery of *well-meaning advice* comes off as condescending or insulting.

You can't control what anyone else thinks or says. You only have control over yourself. With this fact in mind, remember that boundaries are essential. Accept advice that serves you. Politely reject opinions that are unfounded, harmful, or insulting, which can look like you removing yourself from uncomfortable situations, avoiding specific individuals, speaking up when something hurtful is said, or calmly explaining to loved ones why you don't appreciate their opinions at this time.

Right now, you need to prioritize your wellness. Remember to love yourself first and take care of your needs. Everyone else will get over it and be fine.

If a person and their words aren't contributing to your healing and are making things worse for you, then you shouldn't listen to that person. Take the space you need. Cancel plans. Don't worry about upsetting anyone and don't let anyone make this situation about them. This experience is about you. You don't owe anyone your time if they are saying things that make you feel bad. You don't owe anyone a more detailed explanation than "I hear what you're saying, but I respectfully don't want to hear anymore."

If someone doesn't understand why their opinion is harmful and why you need to take space, that's their problem.

You may also have to deal with some of your own limiting beliefs and opinions. During this experience, there's a lot to work through. Unfortunately, you could end up being one of your own worst enemies. You may find yourself fighting off your ideas about how you think your life *should* look.

I'm going to share some of the harmful opinions that I, as well as some of my friends, had to deal with when we were going through our divorces. Some of these opinions came from people in our lives, while other opinions came from ourselves. There were a lot of deeply held beliefs that I had about divorce that I had to work through. A lot of the time, I was my own worst enemy.

To help you cope better than I did, I'm going to give you some tips on how to best deal with harmful opinions that are detrimental to your healing and growth.

"DID YOU GO TO MARRIAGE COUNSELING?"

I had a friend who knew her marriage was over, but she was scared of what other people would think and say to her about it. Instead of ending her marriage when she wanted to (and when she should have), she spent another year in her toxic union. She and her husband had already been going to counseling, but she was so worried about what everyone would think that she made them put in a whole extra year of marriage and an entire year of extra counseling just to hammer home how much their marriage didn't work.

Essentially, she was so afraid of the opinions of other people that she wasted a year of her life in a marriage she knew wouldn't work just to prove how much it didn't work.

Looking back on her journey, her only regret is that she didn't end her marriage earlier. She regrets allowing her fear of the opinions of others dictate what she did with her life.

Maybe you went to counseling and your marriage still didn't work out. Maybe therapy wasn't a saving grace for you and your ex. Maybe your marriage was too broken to be fixed.

At the same time, maybe you didn't go to a single therapy session with your ex. Maybe you knew it wasn't something that would help. There's also a very real possibility that you didn't want to go to therapy. It honestly doesn't matter one bit whether you went or not. Things happened for a reason. And your decision to go to therapy is nobody's business but yours.

If anyone asks if you and your former spouse went to counseling and implies that if you did, you wouldn't be getting divorced, understand that they are projecting their ideas about what needs to happen when a marriage breaks down. Know that their opinion is much more about them than it is about you.

And I'll repeat, your decision to go to marriage counseling is your decision alone.

"MARRIAGE TAKES WORK. YOU DIDN'T TRY HARD ENOUGH . . ."

Another friend of mine heard these exact words from someone who was one of her best friends. Can you imagine? One of your best friends (who, side note, had never even been married herself) standing in front of you, telling you that marriage takes work and that you didn't try hard enough. Like you're some kind of idiot who doesn't know that marriage takes work.

Honestly, my friend was such a sweetheart in this situation. She was mad about what was said, but she did her best to be respectful. I think her response happened because she was so stunned that her friend would even say something like that—a friend who was supposed to be a best friend and support her.

If one of my best friends had said that, I would have responded with something like, "Thanks, Tips," and shot them the biggest eyeroll I had. I would have followed up by telling them exactly where to go and how to get there. But I talk tough now. I give this response as an evolved version of myself that is years removed from my own divorce experience. I give this response as a woman who doesn't take much shit these days. Unfortunately, that's not who I was when I was going through my divorce. The woman I was years ago when I was going through my split was much meeker than who I am today. At the time, if I heard that, I might have responded the same way my friend did.

During your divorce, you might hear this exact statement from well-meaning friends and family. And when you do, it might sting more than you expect, mainly because it's a statement that implies that you didn't take your marriage seriously, you don't understand how much work goes into a marriage, and you didn't try nearly hard enough. Well, let me state this loud and clear so that everyone hears (especially the people at the back):

No one has any idea about what went on behind closed doors between you and your spouse. No one has any right to tell you how much work you did or didn't put into your marriage. No one has any right to tell you that you didn't try hard enough. You know exactly the amount of *trying* you and your spouse did. Don't let anyone tell you otherwise.

There is also a very real possibility that maybe you didn't try that much. Maybe you didn't need to because you knew your marriage wasn't serving you and wouldn't serve you long term. That's perfectly okay. Whatever your story is, you know what is right for you. The decisions you've made have been exactly the right decisions for you. Don't let anyone convince you otherwise.

"YOU CAN'T JUST GIVE UP."

If this opinion comes your way at any point during your divorce, swat it away as fast as you can!

Divorce isn't giving up! Not even a little bit. I would go as far as to say that divorce is the opposite of giving up. It's finally showing up for yourself when you've been neglecting your happiness for far too long. It is choosing what's best for you even though the road is going to be bumpy and challenging.

If someone tells you that divorce is giving up, you can respond this way:

My marriage causes me harm.

Divorce is what's right for me.

Divorce is prioritizing my wellness.

Divorce is the new beginning I need.

Divorce is loving myself the way I deserve.

Divorce is the healing I desperately need.

Divorce will bring me joy and fulfillment.

And if they still don't understand how important divorce is on your journey, hit them with these words: "Divorce is the beginning of everything I dream about."

It's hard for anyone to argue with that.

If at some point you become your own worst enemy and you start to tell yourself that you're giving up because you're getting a divorce, I want you to reread the aforementioned list over and over until you know exactly how much divorce is *not* giving up.

"DIVORCE IS GOING TO RUIN YOU FINANCIALLY."

This opinion isn't completely without merit. I lost all the money I had because of my split. This loss wasn't easy to confront. At the same time, I don't regret my decision. I also have a friend or two who had to declare bankruptcy to pay for their divorce. It did ruin them financially; however, they don't regret their decision to get a divorce. They would do it again, bankruptcy and all, because they're much happier now than they ever were while married.

They'll also be the first to tell you that they could have saved a whole ton of money during their divorce if they had been smarter. I'm not going to go into detail about how to save money during a divorce. There are whole books written about that topic (which I suggest you read). I'll just say that every meeting, every call, every email, and every text with a lawyer is going to cost you money. Keep this fact in mind when communicating with counsel. Every legal battle with your ex will cost you money. Keep this fact in mind when trying to come to agreements.

I recovered financially and both my friends recovered from bankruptcy. It took time, but everyone is back on their feet. Money comes and goes. Your emotional well-being, happiness, and sanity matter much more than any dollar amount. If you are certain that divorce is the best thing for your well-being, then you can't let money get in the way. Anything lost can be made up in the future, including money. Get yourself some financial advice and stand by your decision.

If someone gives you the opinion that your divorce will ruin you financially, thank them for their concern and respectfully let them know you are taking steps to help ease the financial burden. Leave it at that and keep moving forward.

"YOUR EX IS AN ASSHOLE."

After my divorce, I entered the dating scene. I casually dated a man for more than a year. He was a good man who treated me kindly, but he wasn't the right person for me. First of all, I was never in love with him. Second, I probably shouldn't have been dating anyone at that time because I was still healing. But hindsight is 20/20, and I can't do anything to change the past.

A bit of a warning for anyone dating: Just because someone is nice to you and is a good person doesn't mean you should date them long term or pursue a relationship with them.

In reflection, I know I should have ended it sooner, but at the time I was lost, and this casual relationship was filling a void I didn't yet know how to fill myself. Filling this void is no reason to date anyone, but that is how my story played out. Trust me, I've learned from this experience and won't ever do it again.

One issue with the relationship was that this person didn't understand the lasting emotional impact of a divorce. He didn't get it because he had never been through a divorce himself. I'm not saying that you have to go through a divorce to understand divorce, but this man just didn't get it. I'm also not saying that you should only date divorcées, but anyone you date post-divorce should do their best to empathize with your path, your pain, and your healing.

I didn't share much about my ex or my divorce with this man because I didn't want to put any of my issues on him. When I finally felt comfortable giving him a glimpse of my pain, I shared a few tiny pieces of information about why my marriage had failed. His response to this initial disclosure was, and I quote, "I don't know why you're still hung up on that scumbag." It was at that exact moment that I knew I had to stop dating him.

I wasn't "hung up" on my ex. I was being vulnerable and sharing something that had caused me a great deal of pain. Plus, no one is allowed to call my ex-husband names.

Here's the thing: If I choose to, I can call my ex a scumbag, all day and night. I can call him an asshole or a prick (or any other insulting name). I have that privilege because of the very intimate experience we shared together. And I can give that name-calling privilege to friends or family if I choose to. But don't dare call him names without my permission. No one has any right to do that. And a very important note to make is that I don't call him names. I wish him only the best and happiness in his life. So, if I'm not calling him names, some guy I'm dating has no right to go there. Ever.

I have a friend who heard this same type of rhetoric from his friends after his split from his wife. One friend in particular would tell him how much of a "bitch" his ex-wife was. My friend didn't say much in the moment, but he has confided in me how much it hurt.

The reason these statements sting is because it almost feels like a personal attack. We loved our former spouses. We married them. So, what does it say about us if we married a scumbag or an asshole or a bitch?

If anyone in your life is calling your ex names and it bothers you, please take a stand. Don't allow it to continue. It might be a tough conversation, but it's necessary. You need to create boundaries around yourself and communicate what's acceptable. You need to tell people when something makes you uncomfortable or upset. If they are any kind of friend, they will respect your wishes and stop the name calling.

GOD HATES DIVORCE. I'M GOING TO HELL.

Remember when I mentioned that sometimes we can be our own worst enemy? Well, here's a perfect example. The opinion that I was going to hell because I was getting a divorce was completely created by me. The only person who told me this sentiment was the voice inside my head. Personally held beliefs can sometimes be judgmental bitches.

As someone who was baptized and raised Catholic, attended Catholic school, and eventually went on to become a Catholic teacher, I can say with 100 percent conviction that Catholic guilt is a real thing. Apparently, Jewish guilt is also a very real thing (at least that's what a friend told me). Possibly every religion has some sort of guilt built into it.

Anyway, back to this Catholic guilt of mine. It only takes a few minutes of searching around the internet to realize that there's still debate by Catholics about divorce and its status as an "unforgivable sin." The fact that there is even debate in 2021 shows how deep and strong the belief is in the faith. Do you know what else is often viewed as an unforgivable sin? Murder. Somehow, divorce has gotten mixed up in the same category as murder by some Catholics.

Back to that voice inside my head. Early in my divorce, the Catholic guilt had a stronghold on my mind. I had this strange idea that I was going to hell because I was getting a divorce. It was like I had been conditioned, but I honestly have no idea where the conditioning came from. At no point do I ever remember my mom or dad or a priest telling me that I would go to hell if I got a divorce, but for some reason, I believed it to be true.

It took a solid six months of therapy, reading blog posts, and shifting my inner dialogue to convince myself that no, I do NOT have a one-way ticket to the fires of hell because I decided to end my marriage.

The truth that finally set me free from my harmful thinking was that the only thing stronger than any "unforgivable sin" you believe you have committed is a loving higher power that wants you to be happy and to live life to your fullest potential. Any "sin" you believe you are committing may only be a "sin" in your own mind. And possibly, divorce is the opposite of sin because maybe it's exactly what God has planned for you.

"YOU SHOULD STAY TOGETHER FOR THE KIDS."

Other variations of this opinion include:

Divorce will screw up your kids.

Children need to be raised in one home with married parents.

You need to put your wants aside.

Think of the kids.

And on and on and on.

Even though these opinions have been widely debunked by many people, they still linger in popular discourse, in comment feeds on the internet, on the tongues of "experts," and in the opinions of some of our loved ones.

I don't have children with my ex-husband, so I didn't personally hear this opinion during my divorce, but I have friends who did. Speaking on behalf of them and every divorced, single parent out there, **divorce does NOT equal screwed-up kids.**

Just as children can thrive in a two-parent household, they can also thrive in a single-parent household. And the opposite can be said about *screwing up* kids. Children can suffer just as much in a two-parent home as they can in a single-parent home. The makeup of the family does not dictate the mental health and well-being of children.

Does a divorce have the potential to screw up kids? Sure. But it comes down to how the situation is handled by both parents and the environment that's established in the home. If a home is toxic, whether the parents are married or not, the kids will suffer. If the home is peaceful, respectful, and filled with love, the groundwork is there for children to thrive, divorce or not. Kids are resilient. They bounce back. Of course, there may be some tears and therapy required, but that's part of the process. It's much healthier for children to live in a peaceful home free from all the ways you and your ex are toxic.

It is especially true if there's any kind of abuse going on between you and your ex, including physical, emotional, psychological, and verbal abuse. Abuse can have a long-lasting impact on children. If there's any abuse going on in the marriage, even if it's just happening to you, your children are just as much victims as you are. I understand how complicated domestic violence is and how difficult it is to leave, but if there is any abuse happening, I strongly suggest you leave, not just for your sake, but for your children's. DO NOT stay for the kids. By staying, you are doing much more harm than good.

Even if there's no abuse, there are so many other reasons why getting a divorce can be the healthiest choice for the couple and the children involved. Don't let the opinion that you should stay for the kids deter you from moving forward with your divorce. A lot of thought went into your decision. Only you know how essential divorce is for everyone involved, including you, your ex, and your children.

In all honesty, your divorce could end up being the most loving gift you ever give to your children. Give them this gift with your whole heart.

"NO ONE WILL WANT TO DATE A DIVORCÉE OR A SINGLE PARENT."

I was lucky that I never heard this opinion, nor did it cross my mind, but I think this thought can float into the brains of a lot of divorcées.

As already mentioned, sometimes we can be our own worst enemies. We can go down dark paths of insecurities and self-doubt.

There are millions of divorcées looking for love. Dating websites and apps have broken down any stigma that remains about dating post-divorce. And as strange as it sounds, when I was dating, I was actually looking for fellow divorcées. I thought that if we had the divorce experience in common, there could be a deeper level of understanding in our relationship. Of course, I was open to men who had never been married, but there was something appealing about a man who had already done the "big white wedding," the first marriage, and had survived the storm of divorce like I had. So, if I was looking for this type of relationship, there has to be other people out there like me looking to date divorcées.

As far as single parents go, there is something incredibly appealing about someone who has the maturity to care for a child. Just like some people search for divorcées, a lot of people dating (who have never been married, nor have children of their own) are looking to date a single parent.

There may be some people on your dating journey who don't want to date a single parent, but this reality can be applied to so many different dating preferences. Heck, some people don't even want to date blondes (and I say this as a proud blonde). If someone isn't interested in getting to know you, then on to the next!

And to give you a bit of extra encouragement, I know so many people who have met the love of their life after divorce. You have no idea who's waiting for you in your future, just past your fear.

"IT'S GOING TO BE TOO HARD ON YOUR OWN."

Is divorce hard? Of course, it is. It could end up being one of the hardest things you ever face. But *hard* is not the same as *bad* or *toxic*.

Divorce was the hardest thing I've ever gone through, but it was never an experience that was *too* hard. It had the potential to destroy me, but something inside me didn't allow that to happen. I was much stronger than I even knew. I was also much more resilient. I was riding the waves of the worst storm I had ever experienced, yet there I was, getting through the shit.

In the face of all my pain, I rose up and moved through my grief.

As humans, we are built to face really difficult things. Every single day, people survive events that have the potential to destroy them. We rise to the challenge. We fight. We move through the pain. We are created to overcome hardship and pain. Resiliency is literally built into our DNA.

I heard a quote on the show *This Is Us* that perfectly explains how hardships shape us and navigate our path. The character Beth Pearson was reflecting on the advice her dying father gave her about life. In those final moments, he told her, "It's the tragedies that define our lives. They are the fence posts on which the rest of our lives hang."

Divorce was and still is a fence post on my path that changed everything for me. My divorce preceded the greatest awakening of my life to date. It awakened me to exactly what I desired from myself, and a partner, for myself. It awakened in me the desire to build a conscious lifestyle and partnership. It shifted my journey indefinitely, and it was necessary. I needed a profound shift. I needed to wake up. I needed to evolve. I needed the pain, for it was the pain that pushed me to become the woman I'm meant to be. I truly believe my divorce was *written in the stars* because I believe my destiny depended on that event happening. The pain that followed was also just as necessary.

And back to the original opinion that being on your own will be too hard. Well, from my personal experience, being single after my divorce was a huge blessing.

Yes, it was hard to adjust to a new way of life and it was messy, but it was also beautiful.

And I'll take a hard, messy, beautiful existence over unhappiness any day of the week.

If anyone tries to tell you that you aren't strong enough to face this incredibly hard thing, they have no idea who you are. You, my dear, are a warrior, and you will get through it. It has never been and will never be too hard for you because you're stronger than you even know.

"YOU'RE TOO YOUNG TO GET A DIVORCE."

A lot of people who go through a divorce in their twenties or early thirties might hear this statement at some point during the divorce process. I did. Honestly, it was such a weird thing to hear. The statement implies there's some *official* age when divorce becomes okay and acceptable, which just isn't the case. If you're old enough to decide to get married, you're also old enough to decide to get a divorce.

If you know early on in your marriage that it's not going to work, divorcing young, possibly before there are kids or a great deal of finances and shared property, is actually a huge blessing. You'll spend less money on lawyers, have less to split up, and have less to sort out (like child support). You'll also have fewer memories in your short marriage to emotionally work through. If you know early on that you want a divorce, don't stay married for years and years.

While writing this book, I spoke to a woman who was going through a divorce after thirty-five years of marriage. When I asked her about the experience, she told me she was jealous of me and my "young divorce."

She told me, "In my first year of marriage, I already knew it wasn't going to work, but I couldn't leave. It was a different time than it is now. So, I stayed. I spent the next thirty-four years trying to make it work. All the while, I knew that it wasn't right, and I wasn't in love."

One thing you can never get back is time, and that's all she wanted. She wanted her thirty-four years back to live, love, discover, and explore. But nothing can bring back that time. Her experience is a cautionary tale to anyone who knows early on that their marriage isn't going to work. Don't waste thirty-five years of your life staying somewhere because of ideas of obligation and responsibility.

If someone tells you that you're too young to get divorced, please share the story of my dear friend who would give anything to get back the years of her life she spent somewhere she knew she didn't belong.

"IT'S TOO LATE TO START OVER."

On the opposite end of the spectrum is this opinion. This one stings because a lot of divorcées believe it for a really long time, so they waste a lot of that time. They have no idea how to start over, and they think it's impossible and too late for them. So, they stay stuck in unhappy marriages.

The most magical adventures begin when you decide it's never too late.

Your life is in your hands, and you can change at any point. Don't let the opinion that it's too late get anywhere close to you because the future waiting for you, just past uncertainty and doubt, is so beautiful. Don't cheat yourself out of all the magic ahead of you because of your fear.

It's never too late

    to start over

    to discover

    to become

    to change

    to evolve

    to bloom

    to grow

    to love

    to start living life on your terms.

You're Going to Make It.

Your Task

Write about the harmful opinions you've heard during your divorce.

Make sure to also include the harmful personal beliefs you hold. For each one, write how untrue the statement is and why it's untrue for you!

Her world was shattered, and the broken pieces left scars on her soul. Like the warrior she is, she picked up those pieces and built the world she always dreamed about.

@thealexandraevamay

EIGHT

Finding
FORGIVENESS

Like many divorcées, I struggled with forgiveness. I had so much anger and grief that blocked me from moving forward. I clung to it like oxygen I needed to survive, which made it almost impossible for me to forgive my ex and, worse than that, forgive myself.

When I was suffering through it all, I thought I'd never reach healing because it seemed impossible to move forward and push things out of my mind.

During a divorce, a lot of things will come up that will make you extremely angry. A lot of unresolved conflicts, problems in the marriage and issues with your former spouse can, and often do, emerge.

When you were married, even if you were fighting, you at least had your marriage to fight for that could push you toward some desire to try to work things out. When you're going through a divorce, you no longer have a marriage to fight for, so all you're left with is unchecked anger. It can take a long time to sort it out.

I couldn't forgive my ex for his contribution to the destruction of our marriage. Honestly, I blamed the guy for everything. I held onto so much resentment for all the ways I believed he had wronged me and all the ways I thought he had destroyed our marriage.

In all honesty, it wasn't fair to place all the blame on him. There were two people who contributed to the end of our marriage. Two people making mistakes. It wasn't all his fault. I know that now. At the same time, that's not how I felt back then, and I had to work through these feelings. I had to work through all the anger and resentment I felt toward my ex if I hoped to move to the next stage of healing.

Worse than any feelings I had toward my ex were the toxic feelings I had toward myself. I was so angry with myself and went far into the space of toxic self-hate. I said the most horrible things to myself, about myself, all of which came from the guilt I felt for the end of my marriage, for disappointing my family, and for how much of a failure I thought I was.

These were the thoughts that went through my mind daily:

I'm a failure.

I'm damaged.

I'm worthless.

I'm behind in life.

I'll never find love again.

No one is going to want me.

No one is going to love me.

I'm going to be alone forever.

A lot of these toxic thoughts (and for the record, untrue thoughts) were a consequence of me playing the comparison game. I was constantly comparing my life to other people.

I was surrounded by people forming families, getting married, and making babies, and I was over in the corner, waving my hands about, blowing up my life. It was impossible not to feel sad when I thought about how different my life was compared to my peers. I believed I was failing because I wasn't at a certain point in my life. No matter how hard I tried, I couldn't forgive myself for wanting a divorce, which effectively tore my young family into pieces when it seemed like everyone else around me was taking steps to create families. Unfortunately, I think when someone goes through a divorce at any age, it's almost impossible not to compare themself to others.

When I was in that place of comparison and self-blame, I tried my best to forget and move on, but I just couldn't. I couldn't forgive myself for wanting a divorce and walking away. Thoughts and regrets haunted me daily.

I should have stepped out of that comparison game as soon as I entered.

I never should have compared myself to anyone, and neither should you. A big lesson I've learned during this process is that we should never measure how successful we feel in our lives based on any kind of comparison to what anyone else is doing with their life.

If I hoped to heal and move forward, I knew I had to start working toward forgiving my ex and myself, something that took time and some very deliberate steps on my part.

LETTING GO OF THE PAST

The hate-fire that's inside you might be strong enough to burn down a city. Mine was. I was so angry that I couldn't think straight. I was blind to anything good that was happening in my life. It was all-consuming.

My inability to forgive kept me chained to my failed marriage and all that we shared together. I was connected to a man who was no longer physically in my life but who haunted my thoughts daily. I was also handcuffed to the pain that I experienced after the marriage ended.

After hearing thousands of stories from other divorcées through my blog and Instagram, I can say these feelings are fairly standard. Unfortunately, it's these exact feelings that get in the way of authentic forgiveness. Anger is a powerful emotion. It's fueled some of the most iconic characters in literature. Imagine if Hamlet had embraced a more "Zen" approach. He might have been able to forgive that uncle of his.

Want to make forgiveness a priority? One thing you have to do is start letting go of all the anger and resentment that keeps you tied to your past and your pain. I know exactly what you're thinking: *easier said than done.*

Some divorcées have to come to terms with some awful things that happened at the hands of former spouses. Some people have to deal with exes who manipulated, deceived, cheated, controlled, gaslit, and abused. Maybe your ex completely obliterated the marriage vows to honor and cherish. It can be hard to work through it all.

I had my own share of crap to process. I had a lot of anger. I don't think anyone would have blamed me if I had held onto that anger for a lifetime. At the same time, I didn't want to live in that space, and it wasn't healthy for me to go down the rabbit hole of anger. I owed myself more than living in anger for years. I had to love myself more than that.

Emotions are wild and unpredictable, at best. Sometimes, despite our best efforts, we have no control over our feelings. I'm not suggesting that you suddenly become a master of emotional control (or that I suddenly became a master of my emotions the moment I decided to no longer be controlled by them). But there were steps I took during episodes of anger that helped.

When I found myself feeling angry, I would do my best to stop the *rage train* before it left the station. What helped me during my anger was to think about the situation from a different perspective. I did my best to look objectively at situations, which was one of the main strategies that helped me get over my anger. There was no going back in time and changing anything, so I had to look at the past differently if I ever hoped to heal.

Whenever I found myself feeling angry about something, I reminded myself that what happened couldn't be changed but how I felt about it was completely within my control. Essentially, I made a pointed effort to shift my mindset during an angry episode, which helped tremendously.

I also did my best to stop reliving painful memories that were mere shadows in my mind taking up the space that should have been reserved for beautiful new experiences and new memories.

When the painful memories came up, I did my best to spend only a moment reliving them. In fact, I set a limit on how much time I'd allow myself to think about them. I think it was something like five minutes. Then I forced myself to think about my present. I was sick and tired of being stuck and refused to be a hostage to my past. Being anchored into our anger can either serve as fuel to come back into alignment with our soul or it can be the gasoline that destroys our life, if you let it. Which one feels more appealing to you?

I decided to shift my attention to my present and used my anger to imagine my beautiful future. I dedicated mental energy to thoughts of where I wanted my life to go rather than staying fixated on where I had been.

I focused on the joy I wanted in my life moving forward and did my best to leave my pain where it belonged—in the past.

DECIDE TO FORGIVE THE EX

Divorce can leave you feeling totally out of control, mainly because there's so much uncertainty about your future. Whether you believe it or not, one of the things you have 100 percent control over is your choice to forgive.

Whether or not someone has apologized has no bearing on your choice to forgive.

Even if you believe someone's apology isn't genuine or if an apology never actually came, you can choose to forgive. More so, you can choose to let go.

Along my journey, I realized that if I was ever going to find inner peace, I had to choose to forgive my ex for everything I was hanging on to. Even though I felt like I never received a genuine apology, I had to forgive him for any wrongdoing in our marriage that I believed he was responsible for. I had to let go of resentment, anger, and every painful memory that he was part of. Everything I was hanging on to was in the past and couldn't be changed. Hanging on to anger or resentment kept me tied to all the pain I had already experienced.

Even if I didn't realize it at the time, I was choosing to stay stuck. The turning point for me was when I realized that it was in my power to change the word *"couldn't"* into *"wouldn't."* I could forgive him and forgive myself for everything.

It was in my power to choose forgiveness. If I wanted peace in a real way, I had to forgive him and let go, apology or not.

For me, forgiveness was freedom.

It's time for you to make the active decision to let go of your past, as well as the anger and resentment that consumes your thoughts. Even if your ex has never apologized, offer up forgiveness in your heart. Your ex apologizing is out of your control. What you do control is your decision to forgive. If you are able to forgive (even without an apology), your heart can start to let go of some of the anger that fuels your emotions.

If you choose to forgive, you choose freedom for yourself.

CHOOSE TO FORGIVE YOURSELF

More important than any forgiveness you decide to give to your ex is choosing to forgive yourself. You may feel guilt for the demise of your once happy marriage, and you may regret how everything fell apart, but none of that matters. That is in the past. There's no rewind button.

Even if you don't feel you deserve forgiveness, it's time to make the loving choice to stop vilifying yourself.

Forgiving yourself is part of a bigger decision to treat yourself with the same love that you reserve for your friends and family. Choosing to let things go is one of the most significant steps you can take on your journey to achieve healing and self-love. Decide to release your past pains and any personal guilt you feel. It's time to let everything go and start treating yourself with empathy, understanding, and, above all, love. You may reflect on all the ways you could have shown up better in the relationship, but don't ever beat yourself up about it. You were doing the best you could with what you knew, what you had, and who you were at the time.

The best thing I ever did on my journey was making the choice to forgive myself. Meeting myself with grace opened doors of self-acceptance, liberation, and freedom from my past, which helped me make peace with my journey.

Even though I had always imagined a conventional journey for myself that included only one marriage (and definitely no divorce), I realized that it's all right that I was re-routed on a different path. After all, the beauty of life lies in unexpected detours.

It's time to truly forgive yourself and finally breathe a big breath of release. You deserve it!

You're Going to Make It.

Your Task

Write about what is holding you back from forgiveness. Afterward, come up with some ideas of how you can let go of the past and move forward.

You don't have to be a prisoner to your trauma. Instead, your trauma can become a vehicle for transformation and purpose.

@thealexandraevamay

NINE

What I Learned

FROM LOSING JUST ABOUT EVERYTHING

Divorce isn't just the end of a marriage. It's the end of a family, a friendship, and a dream. You often have to say good-bye to friends, property, treasured possessions, money, and for some, a significant amount of time with your children. Not only do you have to come to terms with the end of your married life, but you also have to make peace with losing everything else that comes with it.

During my divorce, I felt like my whole world was being torn apart, piece by piece. In addition to figuring out how to survive the destruction of my marriage, I also had to face losing so many other things.

Did I cope well? Hell no! I was a mess.

Personally, I wasn't ready for the pain. I didn't have the coping skills to deal with losing everything that I ended up losing all at the same time. Consequently, I crumbled, unable to bear it all. Every minute was a struggle. Getting through each day seemed impossible. I was a mere shell of the person I was before the split. I was a mess.

What ended up saving me was my decision to embrace the loss and welcome the pain. If I hoped to start healing in a real way, I had to face everything that had happened. I had to find the value in my loss and accept the pain as an opportunity for knowledge, perspective, and gratitude.

Only when I started accepting each loss as a lesson did I start to happily move forward.

Once I embraced this new perspective, I understood that every loss I suffered was a blessing.

The universe knew I wasn't living my true purpose, so it sent me destruction to open up my life in a magical way where I had endless opportunities. All the things that had been stripped away by the universe, including a home, money, possessions, family, and friends had created the blank space I desperately needed to create the beautiful life I was destined to live. I was now in a position to change everything.

Embracing each loss as a lesson was the most important step in my healing process. From these lessons, I was eventually able to rise from the pain and push through to an entirely new and exciting life. I'm so happy I didn't waste this opportunity for growth.

Let's get to the lessons, shall we?

WHAT I LEARNED FROM LOSING (MORE THAN) ALL MY MONEY

I start my lessons with money because losing a huge sum of it can seem like the most horrible thing to happen. It can feel like your world has completely crumbled; however, throughout this process, I eventually realized that losing my money was actually my most insignificant loss. In fact, it was what needed to happen to re-route my path and shift my overall perspective. Let me explain.

I didn't just lose all my money. Like so many people going through a divorce, I was put into debt. I had worked since I was a teenager, and there I was, in my early thirties, with less than nothing to show for it. It was really difficult to accept.

During this time, I developed even stronger bonds with a few friends who were also going through a divorce. One of my friends was ending her marriage to her husband of more than twenty-five years. We shared the experience of both going through a divorce, but I'm sure that her divorce after twenty-five years was much more significant than what I was experiencing. Her financial hit was also much more significant than my own. Arguably, she would have felt the loss of money much harder.

At the same time, I remember that conversation when she sat across the table from me and told me, with conviction, "It's only money. It comes and goes. Your happiness is the most important."

She was right.

Having no money changes your perspective on what it is to have money. You realize that having all the money in the world is nice, but it doesn't matter nearly as much as being happy. You come to realize that happiness doesn't come from a dollar. Losing everything, even all the cash, was awful. At the same time, it led to the joy I'm living today.

I had to take some measures to get back on my feet. I lived with my parents for a while and then lived with a roommate. I spent less, saved more, spoke with a financial planner, budgeted, and cut up credit cards. I did what needed to be done. Slowly, I started to recoup my losses and realized I wasn't out for the count.

If you are at the part of your journey where all your money has been lost, try not to lose faith. It may take a while, but money can, and most likely will, come back your way. In the meantime, you'll discover some very interesting things about yourself and your relationship with money. As well, you'll discover how financially savvy you are when hard times hit.

WHAT I LEARNED FROM LOSING MY HOME

When we were engaged, my ex and I built a house. We took possession about two months after we were married. It was the first house we owned, and it was beautiful. It was the perfect house and had more than enough room for us and any babies that might have come along. It was also the perfect neighborhood for a newly married couple just starting out. I loved that house.

When we split, one of the first things we talked about was what to do with the house. Neither of us could afford to pay for the house on our own, and neither of us wanted to take on the role of landlord and move in as roommates.

Financially, the only solution was to sell. Emotionally, the only solution was to sell.

For me, our house was a physical representation of the dream we shared to create a life together with family, treasured memories, holidays, celebrations, and everything else. The house represented the promise of a beautiful future together. We also created some wonderful memories during the time we lived there. The house was connected to so much. I couldn't possibly start carving out a new future by myself while still living in the home that represented the future I had planned to create with my ex. Yet, it was still a difficult loss to face.

The house was one of the last possessions that kept us connected.

After the house sold (and it took about seven months on the market), there was nothing physical that we shared. All that was left were the divorce papers.

To help get back on my feet, I relocated to my parents' basement into my childhood bedroom. This move was a hard hit for me. Being in my early thirties and returning to the room I slept in when I was a child felt like an awful full-circle smack from the universe.

At this point, I was too blind to realize that it was a huge blessing. Returning to my childhood home helped me reconnect with the person I was before all the trauma and grief had set in. Being back in that bedroom reminded me that even though I had lost my way, the person I once was still lived inside me. I was reminded of that girl whose personal mantra used to be *things always work out. Maybe they don't work out exactly as you planned, but things work out.*

And things have worked out, in the most beautiful way.

Even though houses are attached to dreams and memories, please remember that a house is just a house. It only has as much emotional value as you place on it. If you are able to remove sentiment and emotion from your house, it becomes just a thing. It isn't a dream or a beautiful future. In a divorce, it's just another possession you might need to get rid of to start the next chapter.

Most importantly, you will make new dreams in new houses. I know this because I already have.

WHAT I LEARNED FROM LOSING FRIENDS

I'm fortunate to have very fierce, loyal friends. My home team is strong. We've seen each other through breakups, job losses, critical illnesses, deaths of family members, new homes, babies, marriages, and divorces. Throughout my split, my friends stuck by my side. This section isn't about them. They are amazing! If any of them are reading these words, I love you very much.

The friends I lost during my divorce were some of the mutual friends that my ex and I had made during our years together. When you go through a divorce, you're fooling yourself if you think everyone will remain neutral. People will pick sides. It's just the nature of the beast. When my split happened, most of our mutual friends picked his side.

When I reflected on why this happened, I had a huge realization. A lot of our relationship and marriage were spent living *his* life.

We rented the apartment he found and wanted. We bought the house he wanted. We lived in the neighborhood he picked. The mutual friends we spent most of our time with, together as a couple, were his friends. I'm by no means trying to paint myself as some kind of victim, because I happily went along with this dynamic; however, it was still the reality (and a reality I didn't fully realize until after we split).

When we split and the side-taking happened, these "mutual"

friends picked his side, which honestly was to be completely expected. They were his friends. What kind of friends would they be to him if they didn't pick his side? Either way, when the dust settled and everyone had aligned themselves with him or me, there were fewer people in my circle.

What did I learn from it? First off, losing some of these people in my life wasn't a loss at all. Some of the friends that fell by the wayside aren't necessarily the people I would choose to spend time with on my own. The second thing I learned was that I prefer having a few very close friends as opposed to a large circle of acquaintances. I also learned that the universe has a funny way of bringing new friends into your life when other friendships end—which is exactly what happened to me.

WHAT I LEARNED FROM LOSING FAMILY

Some of you may think it's strange for me to mention grief over in-laws. There are many stories of awful in-laws out there, and there are many people who are happy to be free of them. On the other side, there are just as many stories of people who loved their in-laws. This section is for you.

Throughout my entire relationship with my ex, I spent a lot of time with my in-laws. I have so many fond memories of evenings spent with them, playing with the kids, and soaking up the sun in the backyard. I remember meals shared and outings. I attended birthday parties, Christmas mornings, and weddings. I received the family calendar and had a lot of shared experiences.

When the split happened, I had to make peace with losing all these people from my life and accept that I was losing half my family.

At first, the loss didn't make an impact. It was kind of like the experience of mourning a death: I didn't feel it automatically, something that went on for quite some time. And then one day, it all just hit me, and the emotional floodgates opened. The reality that I had lost all these people from my life swept over. Letting them go wasn't easy. The loss was really hard. I missed them a lot.

Unfortunately, there's nothing you can do about losing your ex's family from your life. It's horrible, but it's part of a divorce. There's no quick fix or easy way to move past it. You just have to accept and have faith. When you think about them, send them some light and love and let it go.

The biggest lesson I can give you about losing in-laws is that sometimes, despite your best efforts, you will lose people you love, and it will hurt. The pain won't last forever, however.

WHAT I LEARNED FROM LOSING MY BEST FRIEND

My ex-husband was my best friend. It's important to note that I don't claim the whole *best friend* title lightly. Most people are best friends with their spouse. That is territory that comes with being married; however, we truly were best friends, with or without marriage. I honestly believe we would have been best friends without all the relationship and marriage stuff. That man could make me laugh like no other. Our friendship was always one of the strongest aspects of our relationship.

Ending my marriage meant saying good-bye to my best friend.

It took me a long time to make peace with that. It was one of the hardest losses for me to grieve. Early on, it came up in therapy a lot: how much I missed my friendship with him. My therapist would ask if I could somehow salvage the friendship because I missed it so much, but I knew that wasn't possible. There was too much water under the figurative bridge. I had to move forward without my best friend.

At the same time, life is full of unexpected experiences and relationships with new people. After splitting with my ex, I quickly realized that I have so many amazing people in my life and best friends whom I love dearly. These wonderful humans are my joy and happiness. They are also my future. These people have filled up my heart.

If you're struggling with the loss of your best friend, my biggest piece of advice is to fill the void by spending as much time as you can with friends and loved ones. Open your heart to the possibility of new friendships. Trust that the universe will bring the right people to you at the right time to help fill the hole you may be feeling right now. Trust that you will find a new best friend.

In the meantime, love yourself so much that you become your own best friend.

WHAT I LEARNED FROM LOSING A MARRIAGE

Losing my marriage was the most devastating experience of my life. You could argue this whole book shows just how hard it was for me. You're right. It rocked me to my core and led me to the darkest place of my life. At the same time, it was also the most transformative and valuable experience I've ever been through.

My true path wasn't to stay in my first marriage. Divorce was the ground-shattering experience that I needed to shake up my life. And perhaps for you, it is the same.

My journey needed to be re-routed to arrive at my awakening.

Unfortunately, it took a long time to come to that realization and understanding. I went through at least a year of guilt, shame, and depression before I emerged from my divorce-induced *grief fog*.

When I did emerge, it wasn't exactly a phoenix-from-the-ashes situation, as I wasn't nearly strong enough to label myself a phoenix, but I had risen from the ashes of my life and a transformation had occurred. It's almost impossible not to transform when your whole life crashes to the ground and all that's left is a weakened soul just trying to survive.

I learned a lot from losing not just my marriage but also losing everything else:

- Grief is messy.
- Mental health should be taken seriously.
- Even the most permanent things can change.
- I wasn't the best partner I could have been.
- There are things that can forever leave a scar on your soul.
- No matter the tragedy, life goes on.
- The only things certain in life really are death and taxes.
- The journey of life is a lot more complex than I ever imagined.
- I'm a lot stronger than I ever thought.

I've saved the biggest and most important lesson for last. In the end, if you take nothing else from this book, know this fact: Healing is possible.

You're Going to Make It.

Your Task

It's your turn to write down the lessons you've learned so far along your healing journey.

Feel free to use mine, but don't shy away from the lessons that are just yours.

I used
to live our life.
Now I live mine.

TEN

Another Fucking
GROWTH OPPORTUNITY

Now that I have connected with literally thousands of divorcées from every walk of life, I know two things to be true:

- Divorce doesn't discriminate against anyone of any age, race, religion, socioeconomic status, sexual orientation, or gender.
- Most people don't believe that divorce will be part of their journey.

Everyone I've spoken with has told me they got married with the right intentions: *'til death do us part*. Some had reservations heading into the union and knew there were red flags, but I have yet to meet a divorcée who admits that on the day they got married they also expected to be divorced. At the same time, they ended up exactly where they didn't expect to be.

Don't tell happily married folk, but divorce can happen to anyone.

I never thought divorce could happen to me. After all, I had done everything right: I dated a man for the *appropriate* three to four years before getting engaged, did a marriage prep course, had the big wedding, and bought a beautiful house in the suburbs. I was following *the steps*: the ones we see in movies and in the lives of people we know. The steps we are applauded for in society.

My life was on course, or at least that's what I believed. Never in a million years did I think I would go through a divorce. I didn't believe that it could happen to me, especially at a relatively young age. It seemed impossible that life had taken such a drastic turn. I would later realize how immature my thinking had been.

This *truth* about my immunity to divorce, which I had held dear to my heart for my whole life, made it extremely difficult to accept my split when it happened, which ended up being extremely detrimental to my personal growth and development.

Even though *I* chose to end my marriage, I perceived my divorce as a horrible thing that was happening *to me* that I had little control over.

In a way, I had unwittingly and psychologically removed myself from my divorce, which resulted in two unfortunate consequences. First, I held myself back from taking any accountability for my part in the divorce. Second, because I unconsciously viewed the divorce as something happening to me and not something I was a part of, it was as if my healing and happiness were out of my hands. This seeming lack of control blocked me from actively loving myself enough to seek out happiness.

I was blind to the reality that was unfolding in front of me. A new path had formed; however, I had yet to consciously walk the trail. I had yet to step into my awakening that had already been set in motion.

Yes, I was coping with one of the hardest experiences of my life, but it wasn't all doom and gloom. My fixation on the negative held me back from truly embracing the new journey that was happening in my life. Doors were opening, people were coming into my life, relationships were being formed, and new lessons were there for the learning. Unfortunately, I didn't see any of it. Instead, I chained myself to memories of my past, drowned in the waves of grief, and turned a blind eye to the real possibilities that were opening up in my life.

Honestly, I enabled my suffering.

My therapist was a firsthand witness to the negativity that was spewing out of every pore of my body. She was there when I was crushed by grief, she was the primary witness when I was spiraling out of control under the impact of trauma, and she had a front-row seat for my depression.

Thinking back, I'm sure it was probably tiring for her to listen to it all, but she never showed anything but comfort and understanding. She sat through every session and listened to my complex set of emotions and thoughts, greeting each with only empathy and compassion. Thankfully, for me, it was my wonderful therapist who helped me snap out of my funk. She shined a light straight into my darkness when she reminded me that divorce is more than just grief and trauma.

During one of my therapy sessions, she explained to me that I could shift my mindset if I viewed my divorce as *Another Fucking Growth Opportunity*.

What a huge wake-up call! Up until this point, I had just viewed divorce as an experience that brought much destruction to my life. In reality, this destruction created an amazing opportunity to grow and transform. Divorce is heartbreaking, but it is also a deeply personal, life-altering, ground-shaking experience that is, at its core, another fucking growth opportunity.

After a divorce, there really is only one direction to take—onward.

Growth is inevitable. You will grow, you will break, you will bloom exactly where you have been planted. And you will rise. The only way to go up, is up.

During this process, I discovered that there were parts of my personality lying dormant. In attempts to be a good partner, I had always put my ex's needs and wants first. I sacrificed pieces of myself to ensure that he was happy, behavior that was extremely toxic. And it wasn't just something I did for him. I had spent my entire adult life in one romantic relationship or another, losing myself or changing aspects of my personality to accommodate someone else. You might as well have nicknamed me chameleon!

Divorce forced me to examine my unhealthy patterns. If I ever wanted to have a healthy relationship with someone else, I had to grow. More importantly, if I ever hoped to have a healthy relationship with myself, I had to grow.

I had to stop prioritizing the happiness of others ahead of my own. I had to stop hiding precious pieces of myself from those I loved out of fear they wouldn't accept me. I finally started to understand that I didn't need to change myself for someone else to love me.

Without any romantic distractions, I finally had the space I needed to fully realize who I was, inside and out, independent from any relationship, which forced me to wholeheartedly accept myself, flaws and all. I realized that the only way to have an authentic experience on this earth was to *be* truly authentic. This realization forced me to finally be unabashedly exactly who I am. I started showing up for my life as my true self and made no apologies for it.

This transformation was more powerful than any change of

behavior I made to be a good partner to someone else because this change happened so that I could be a good partner to myself.

I finally started to love myself first.

Throughout this process, I learned how to take care of myself, all by myself. I was one of those women who moved straight from her parents' home into her husband's home. Thus, I had never known what it was like to live by myself and keep myself company. I didn't know how to emotionally support myself during hard times. I hadn't developed authentic coping strategies for hardships because I had never faced hardship on my own. There had always been someone taking care of me. For the first time in my life, I finally had to learn how to do everything by myself.

During this time, I learned how to sell a house, find a place to live, take care of a car, have difficult conversations, take care of my finances, cook, stand on my own two feet, move, change jobs, be my own best friend, spend a weekend with only myself as company, and cuddle myself to sleep. It was all extremely liberating!

This newfound independence drove me to reach for dreams that I had possibly pushed aside, as I had believed them to be somewhat out of reach.

I have been fortunate in my life, specifically with travel. I've seen quite a bit of this world. I've been lucky enough to travel to more than twenty-five countries. Some of my travel experiences include three weeks eating pasta and drinking espresso in Rome, two months traveling all over Western Europe, and a six-week adventure exploring Southeast Asia. Despite all this travel, I had never yet traveled in the ways I always dreamed I would: with my sister and as a solo traveler.

My newfound mission to show up as my authentic self meant I couldn't push aside my travel dreams anymore.

Two years after I split from my husband, I finally went on the trip that would heal the brokenness that was still inside my heart. That summer, my beautiful sister and I embarked on a journey through Portugal and Spain. We didn't know what we were doing, we lost our luggage for more than a week, and we got separated and lost a time or two, but it was the most magical trip of my life. Being with my sister in such a beautiful place reminded me of the light that still existed in my life and that my future could be bright and filled with joy.

After my sister returned home to Canada, I found myself all alone, boarding a plane to Greece, embarking on the solo adventure I had always dreamed about. While exploring Santorini, Mykonos, and Ios, I ate gyros every day, laughed with locals about my Canadian accent, and explored the birthplace of democracy. It was there that I also made a new best friend who I can honestly say will be a lifelong friend.

My bucket list had one more item checked off it, and I couldn't be more thankful. It's difficult to truly explain what this trip meant to me, but I can say with full certainty that my "sister adventure" and "solo adventure" were the most extraordinary gifts I've ever given to myself.

Travel wasn't the only dream I chased.

Divorce was the trigger that uncovered other unrealized passions. And if I'm going to be specific, it was actually the grief of divorce. Let me explain. If I hadn't suffered such extreme grief, I never would have turned to writing as an outlet. When I started to write, something sparked deep inside my soul. Releasing my pain onto the page opened doors within me I didn't know existed. The words poured out of me, and with every one, I started to feel more and more like myself. I also started the most incredible journey of my life to date and began walking the path that destiny always had planned for me.

Through my writing, I started a blog, found an amazing community of incredible souls, made deep friendships, connected with people around the world, became an advocate for mental health, joined organizations with incredible people advocating for important causes, wrote a book, and shifted the course of my life forever.

My divorce ended up being an amazing vehicle for growth, development, and, ultimately, transformation. It pushed me closer to the path I was destined to walk. If I had never experienced it, I would have never gotten to know the person I am at my core. I'm not sure I ever would have attained true happiness, peace, and contentment.

My divorce was not a life sentence of pain but rather an amazing gift given to me by the universe to truly discover who I am and what I want.

And I plan on cherishing every moment!

You're Going to Make It.

Your Task

Write a list of all the ways you've grown and all the blessings that have come into your life since your split.

- Have you discovered a new passion?
- Switched careers?
- Traveled?
- Fallen in love?
- Discovered who you truly are?
- Gained a new understanding of how independent you can be?
- Learned how to take care of yourself?

Dig deep and be authentic about your personal growth on this journey so far.

If your divorce broke you, it's time to rise up and show the world the masterpiece you've become.

@thealexandraevamay

ELEVEN

Loving
YOURSELF AGAIN

Divorce isn't kind. In fact, it's downright mean. It beats you up and forces you to your knees. It's an ever-present, daily force that infiltrates every aspect of your life and finds your weaknesses.

Personal insecurities rise
Loneliness sweeps in.
And you're stuck in the middle, just trying to keep it together.

It can be challenging to love yourself in the best of times, so when life throws you to the ground, self-love can feel impossible. Rebuilding yourself after divorce isn't easy and won't happen overnight. It's going to take work, healing, and time. And even if you work at it and you're in a wonderful place in your life, loving yourself can, at times, seem hopeless. Insecurities get in the way. Personal expectations can be harmful. Comparison is the enemy. Uncertainty and anxiety can disrupt everything.

Loving yourself through divorce can be one of the hardest tasks you do. However, even among all the pain, challenges, and grief, there is light and opportunity. Divorce creates a chasm in your life, opening a blank space to fully understand, love, and accept who you truly are. You are not broken—you are being given an opportunity to rebuild yourself stronger, better, more YOU than ever before.

At the end of it, you will love yourself greater than you ever have, which is truly the most valuable gift you can give yourself.

After the end of my marriage, I realized that the only way to heal the mountain of my emotional wreckage was to heal it exactly how it was built: piece by piece. It's taken a lot of work, healing, and time to get to a place where I can say without any reservation, "I love the shit out of myself," but I did it. I want the same for you.

Radical acceptance of yourself and unwavering love starts here.

PRIORITIZE SELF-CARE

For a long time, I didn't take self-care seriously. In my limited understanding, I believed that it was an indulgent practice. To me, self-care was a day at the spa, or getting a haircut, or having a bubble bath, or participating in girls' nights. I understood self-care as going after the things I wanted and desired, whatever those may be. It seemed selfish. Boy was I wrong!

Self-care is the practice that opens up the road to you being the best version of yourself. It encompasses a way of living and should be an integral part of your day-to-day habits.

The first step on your self-care journey is to be fully accepting that self-care is a practice of addressing what your mind, body, and soul need to be healthy, happy, balanced, and at peace. Whether we are fully aware of it or not, we all practice self-care by doing things to achieve balance and wellness in our lives. When you take a nap in the afternoon, say no to plans because you want to spend the evening alone, or go for a run after work to decompress, you are practicing self-care.

Self-care doesn't need to look or be glamorous, it just needs to feel nourishing and true to you.

For example, I may want that extra glass of wine at dinner because I've had a hard day emotionally, but that may not be what my body needs that day. The extra glass of wine may taste delicious and help me unwind, but I know that if I drink it, I probably won't have a good sleep and my scalp psoriasis could flare up. At that moment, the wine is what I want, but it's not necessarily what I need. Self-care in that situation is weighing my wants and needs and making the decision accordingly. Do I indulge and drink wine from time to time? For sure! But I always make sure to check in with myself. Am I sacrificing my health, balance, and peace? If I find I'm sacrificing one of those things, then whatever I desire at that moment is not self-care but more of a "want."

Self-care was paramount for me during my divorce and became my saving grace when I was trying to adapt to my new life. Making self-care a priority (which was to make my needs and wellness a priority) forced me to get out of bed on the days I wanted to stay in a dark room under the covers. I knew that my mental health depended on doing something with my day, even if that was as simple as making breakfast, taking a shower, and reading the news. Prioritizing self-care helped me not fall to pieces on days when I thought I would crumble under grief. It was the vehicle that helped me move into a healthy emotional space and start to love myself again.

My self-care list during my divorce:

- Attending therapy
- Getting enough sleep
- Practicing yoga
- Journaling
- Spending time in nature
- Taking a shower or bath before bed
- Spending time with family and friends
- Taking breaks from social media
- Listening to music I love
- Eating well
- Working out
- Connecting with others living through the same experience
- Making time for girls' nights
- Taking weekends away with friends
- Reading inspiring quotes
- Using essential oils and aromatherapy
- Treating myself as kindly as I treated those I love

During your divorce, self-care may be the thing that makes the difference between self-love and long-term suffering. You may not see an immediate benefit, but if you stick with it, you may be surprised by how much healing can be ushered in when you make *YOU* a priority.

TAKE BREAKS FROM SOCIAL MEDIA

After my husband and I split, every time I saw a friend post on Instagram that they got married, I became a mess. Every time I opened another post that showed someone living their best life, I felt awful about all the shit going on in my own. There were all these people around me doing incredible things, and I was blowing up my life. Taking breaks from social media was exactly what I needed. These breaks gave me space to stop the endless comparison that I was doing. I stopped looking at other people and started focusing on myself and the beauty that still surrounded me. Even if some of my life was messy and sad, I gained an appreciation for the many wonderful aspects that were still there. I stepped out of the race (that I never wanted to be part of) that I had somehow found myself in.

Even though we know people only post the highlight reel, the reel can still make us feel shitty about our own lives. You are going to lose every single time you compare your life to anyone on social media, which is a compilation of the very best moments of that person's life. It's time to put down your phone, stop scrolling through Instagram, log out of Facebook and get off Twitter or any other social media platform you use.

It's time to stop chasing the highlight reel and start appreciating the beautiful moments in your life (even if your life is a bit messy).

CHANGE YOUR INTERNAL DIALOGUE

During a divorce, even the strongest individuals can slip into a pattern of thinking damaging thoughts. There's nothing quite like a divorce to destroy self-worth and confidence. If you are anything like I was, on any given day there is a steady stream of negative self-talk going on inside your mind.

When I found myself suddenly single, my confidence was at an all-time low. I felt like a failure and hated how life had unfolded. Unfortunately, I was beating myself up mentally every single day and degrading my self-worth more than I ever deserved. It was easy for me to go down the road of self-hatred when I was swimming in the ocean of grief and struggling with the waves of trauma.

If you had looked into my mind on any given day during my divorce, you would have seen a stream of damaging self-talk, including statements like *I'm broken, I won't survive this, I deserve to be alone.*

Thoughts become things. *The more I thought about these incredibly harmful ideas, the more they took root in my mind.*

These phrases became my story.

To rewrite my internal dialogue, I had to take a hard look in the mirror and be real with myself. I was the only one treating myself horribly and verbally abusing myself every single day. I was my worst enemy. I was the villain in my life. There was no one to blame but me.

A turning point was when I realized I deserved to treat myself as kindly as I treated those I love. I deserved self-love and respect. I deserved the same treatment I was giving everyone else in my life.

I had to take responsibility for my thoughts and change the dialogue going on in my mind. I would never move past the hole of self-hatred if I continued to dig the hole. I used all my strength to move past the phrases that were slowly destroying me and learned how to love myself again, word by word.

It was hard at first, mainly because negative self-speak had become a habit. Self-love isn't necessarily organic. You must be intentional about it and nourish your positive thoughts, words, and actions.

For example, I had to be intentional and make myself say words of acceptance every day. No matter what, I made the effort to give myself at least one compliment in the morning and one before bed. It felt unnatural at first; eventually, however, the compliments came more easily. I complimented myself on the good days and on days I couldn't think of anything nice to say to myself, which were the days I needed it the most.

Once I forced this shift, self-love became easier because I had less room in my mind for negative self-speak. Every day, I found new things to love about myself. This practice started to flow into the rest of my day. The compliments were coming all day instead of just during the scheduled morning and evening self-love boost. What had seemed impossible at first was actually always inside me, yearning to get out. It was a train that couldn't be stopped. It was the vehicle that helped me fall in love with myself all over again. My words of self-hatred had been replaced by words of love.

Changing my internal dialogue through a practice of positive, loving self-talk and compliments helped save me.

Don't get me wrong, there were still days when I started going down the road of destructive thinking. However, I would allow myself to live in a negative headspace for only five minutes. After the five minutes were up, I didn't allow myself to think another harmful thought about myself. Eventually, the negativity became less and less as self-love started to dominate my thoughts.

That is my hope for you: to have a mind that is dominated by strong, unwavering, beautiful thoughts of endless self-love.

BE INTENTIONAL WITH HOW YOU SPEND YOUR TIME AND WHO YOU ALLOW INTO YOUR UNIVERSE

When I was newly single, I did whatever I wanted, whenever I wanted. And a lot of the time I wasn't thinking about what was best for me. Instead, I was doing whatever I wanted in a haphazard way, engaging in my fair share of self-destructive behaviors. Reflecting now, I should have been more intentional with my time, doing more things to help myself heal.

When a marriage ends, it can be easy to fill your free time with destructive behaviors that feel good and momentarily take your mind off things. Instead, make time for things that fill up your self-care list. Don't neglect your therapy appointments or spend every weekend in bed, crying under the covers. Make time for journaling, meditation, and your weekly yoga class. Invest in the art class you've always wanted to take. Be intentional with your time so that you're prioritizing activities that will help you heal.

Prioritizing time either with people I loved or by myself and doing things I enjoyed on a regular basis magically grew my self-love. Investing my time in growing my relationship with others helped to funnel love into a relationship with myself.

Just as important as saying yes to plans with people you love is saying no to toxic friends and family. There's no shame in saying no to plans with people who don't serve you or your vision of how you want your life to look. Enforcing boundaries is more than just healthy, it's necessary. It is okay to end friendships. I did. It was really hard, but it was also extremely necessary for the direction I wanted for my life. I no longer had time or energy for toxic friendships or relationships. I hope you have enough strength and conviction to do the same for yourself.

Make joy and peace your goal.

If something or someone brings you joy, follow it with every ounce of your being. Hold those people close. If something brings you peace, do everything you can to pursue it. These are things that will save you in the end.

If there's anyone in your life who's criticizing your choices, ignore them. Right now, you owe it to yourself to do exactly what you need to do to become the person you know you're destined to be.

DATE YOURSELF ONCE A WEEK

Yes, just like you dated your ex when you first met, date yourself. Pamper yourself. Get curious, explore new places, try new things. Every time you achieve a level of self-love and acceptance, a new layer of yourself is uncovered. You then have to continue the process to accept this new layer. It never really stops. It's a lifelong journey. Dating yourself will help you continually discover who you truly are, week after week, month after month, and year after year. Every time you uncover a new layer of yourself, you have another date to continue to fall in love with yourself in a way you haven't before.

It's time to get to know yourself again and figure out what you want and what makes you feel good.

The first step is to become aware of how you feel when you do things. Do you feel exhausted at work but exhilarated when you are reading? Do you feel joy when you are playing with your children?

Are you fulfilled when you are writing in your journal? Do you look forward to volunteering?

The more that you do the activities you love, the happier you'll be. And if that means you have to say no to other plans, so be it. Perhaps you need to rearrange your schedule so that you can go for a walk in the river valley every day to recharge. Maybe you need to save some money to buy a new camera so you can join the photography class you've always wanted to be part of. Perhaps you want to join a sports team or a club of like-minded people. Do whatever you need right now to be you.

Make the time to date yourself at least once a week. These dates don't have to be extravagant nights out. Dating yourself could be as simple as making your favorite meal, enjoying an extra-long bubble bath, watching your favorite movie, or reading a new book. Becoming single can wake things inside you that you never anticipated. The person you are after a divorce could be very different from the person you were in your former marriage. There is no better way to tackle loneliness and celebrate this exciting new chapter than by fully loving and appreciating the amazing person you are!

On your date nights, say these self-love truth bombs out loud:

> *I'm special.*
> *I'm powerful.*

I'm beautiful.

I'm important.

I'm magnificent.

I'm worthy of joy.

I deserve a beautiful life.

I always have the company of ME.

I'm free to create the life of my dreams.

I'm stronger than any struggle that comes my way.

Your divorce happened for a reason that you may not even fully understand yet. This experience is a stepping-stone that is needed to lead you to where you're going. You have no idea of the opportunities and adventures that await and the beauty that's to come. Hold on tight because joy is going to reveal itself!

And until that joy forms organically, remind yourself every day that you're worthy of the incredible, beautiful, extraordinary life that's waiting for you!

You're Going to Make It.

Your Task

What's on your self-care list?

Take time to make your very own self-care list of all the things you need in your life.

- How can you create time and space for them?

I was married.
And then I wasn't.
My heart shattered
in a way that was
impossible to piece
back together. The
grief was suffocating.
The darkness made
it impossible to see
any light. Despite this, I
healed. So can you.

@thealexandraevamay

TWELVE

Decluttering
YOUR LIFE OF ALL THE THINGS

After my marriage ended, I had to decide what to do with a lot of things. I had so many relationship mementos: postcards from trips we had taken, jewelry, letters, cards, knickknacks, gifts, books, and photographs.

I wasn't married anymore, yet my house was filled with many things that kept me trapped in my past.

Items take up physical space in a house and a great deal of mental, spiritual, and emotional space inside us. Plus, they carry energy and memories. My marriage had ended, and I was trying to move forward, yet the photo album sitting on the bookshelf with pictures from the first trip we took made it nearly impossible. If I wanted to move forward authentically and make space for new things to enter my life, I had to get rid of a ton of items.

When I first started decluttering, I was extremely overwhelmed by the process. Deciding what to keep and what to chuck was a daunting task. I had developed strong emotional attachments to a lot of things, and it was difficult to break those ties. I was scared that getting rid of items that we had held so dear as a couple would somehow be disrespectful to the relationship and love we had shared. But the truth was the opposite.

Decluttering my space resulted in a profound amount of healing, and it was the exact step I needed to take.

When I removed items from my life that were connected to my past, I found it easier to detach from my marriage. It also made room in my heart for new things, people, and experiences. I was starting a new chapter, and it was important to begin with an open heart. I suggest the same to you!

When you're reevaluating your possessions, you might find yourself thinking:

> *Where do I start?*
> *How am I going to part with this item?*

How am I going to let go?

What do I do with everything?

It can cause a ton of anxiety!

To ease your mind, address each question individually. I like making lists. Maybe you need to answer each question on a piece of paper. This process can help you work through it all and reduce stress.

My suggestion (which is nothing new) is to make different piles: *Keep, Give Away, Sell,* and *Throw Away.* Be ruthless. Make sure you are getting rid of more than what you're keeping. When contemplating anything, try to push sentiment out of your mind. And if pushing the sentiment feels hard, pause, take a deep breath, and give thanks for that memory or sentiment and release it with love. When we release things with love, we leave more room for love and joy to enter our lives.

Do you really need to keep the cake server you used at your wedding reception that has your initials engraved in it? Probably not. Do you need the lamp you bought because your ex liked it? Definitely not.

Once you've sorted all items into the four piles, go to bed. Leave the piles for a couple of days. Then return to them and have another look. Something you should be throwing away may have somehow ended up in the keep pile. Taking a few days to rest between sorting and reevaluating your choices will help you gain a new perspective that only a new day can provide. I also suggest you invite a close friend or family member over to evaluate your choices. They may provide a different, more ruthless perspective.

Most likely there'll be some mementos you know you should part with but aren't ready to give away or throw away . . . just yet. You don't need to get rid of these items right away, but you do need to get them out of your space. *Out of sight, out of mind* applies so well in this situation. Box up these items and put this box somewhere out of sight. Maybe store it in a friend's closet or a storage locker. You'll get the items out of your home, making it less likely that you'll open the box during moments of emotional weakness.

In a year, take the box out and decide whether you need to open it or if you can just put the whole box in the garbage unopened. My hope for you is that the box goes straight into the trash. If you do feel compelled to open it, make sure you have a bonfire close by, ready to burn anything you're ready to get rid of. Burning these items will hopefully be the last cathartic action you need to fully let these mementos go.

If you have things to give away or sell, there are some great companies and organizations that cater to people who are going through a divorce. A quick search on the internet can help you find a local company that can help you.

Divorce is the perfect opportunity to reevaluate everything in your life. It's time to start purging!

THINGS TO GET RID OF

Bedsheets

Your white linen sheets may be the most comfortable sheets in the world or cost hundreds of dollars, and they may have the highest thread count and feel oh so soft, but reality check, hello! You slept on them with your ex. Why would you want to sleep another night on them? It may have cost you a ton of money to buy your sheets, but they are one of the first things you should get rid of after a divorce. Get rid of them early in the separation. You can throw them out, give them away, sell them—it doesn't really matter. Just get them gone. There are too many memories as well as a lot of bad energy trapped in those sheets.

Gifts from Your Ex

Even if the gift doesn't stir up an emotional reaction right now, it could one day cause a storm of tears when you least expect it. We connect a lot of emotions and memories to items (even if we don't recognize it). Gifts can be huge triggers for reminding you of happy times. They can make you doubt your decision to end your marriage. You don't need these reminders in your life. Trust that you made the right choice for your overall well-being to leave the relationship.

I had a hard time throwing out gifts or getting rid of them in the beginning. So, I boxed them up. At the very least, I needed to get them out of my space. I moved them to storage and instantly felt more removed from my marriage. Like I mentioned, *out of sight, out of mind*. When I finally felt ready, I returned to the box and dealt with the gifts.

Souvenirs

You've possibly accumulated a lot of souvenirs from your time with your ex from different trips you took together, events you attended, and adventures you experienced. Now is the time to purge this stuff! Even if it was the best concert you ever attended or the most amazing trip to Europe, you have to be real with yourself when making these decisions.

Are you able to separate the experience from your memories of your ex? If the answer is yes, then I guess the T-shirt can stay. If the answer is no, then you already know what you need to do.

Any Home Decor Items That Remind You of Your Ex

Did your ex choose the painting hanging in the entryway? Did you pick out dishes together? Did you buy specific bedside lamps with your ex in mind? Is the house decorated based on your ex's taste? It may be time to get rid of a lot of furniture and other decor items in your house.

Your home should be your sanctuary. If certain furniture, decor pieces, and art are getting in the way of internal peace, it's time to consider selling those things and buying something new. It is your chance to start fresh with new pieces that make you only feel happy!

Any Wedding Items (Including Your Dress)

Do you still have that card box from your wedding or the thirty vases you used for centerpieces? If so, it's time to box those things up and start selling. Even if they're beautiful, there's no need to hang onto anything that makes you think about your wedding day. When you are getting divorced, the last thing you want to be reminded of or think about is the one day when you were the most hopeful for a lifelong marriage.

The most important item to part with (and for many, the most difficult) is your wedding dress. Even if it was the dress of your dreams and the most beautiful gown you've ever worn, if you want to move on in any real way, you can't have your wedding gown hanging in the back of your closet. It has to go! It is time to get rid of the piece of clothing that is the ultimate symbol of your wedding day. It might seem impossible, but I promise that you'll feel so much better once you do it!

There are many budget-conscious brides out there who would love to get their hands on second-hand items for their big day. You can sell anything wedding related online, including your dress. There are many buy-and-sell websites and marketplaces for wedding items that make the process super simple.

You may be thinking, *What if I get married again and want to use these things?* If you find yourself getting married again, I guarantee you won't want to use anything from your first wedding.

Photos

In an ideal world, you'd be able to throw out all the photos in one big purge; however, I know it isn't necessarily that simple. For me, photos were the hardest items to let go. I had a difficult time getting rid of photos for a really long time. So, if you're struggling, I get it!

If you are committed to throwing out all the photos but find that you can't do it in one big purge, do it in steps. Set a goal for yourself every month to throw out a few until the day you find that you're free from them all.

If you can't bring yourself to throw out photos, then do what I did initially. In the beginning, I wasn't emotionally ready to deal with the photos. So, I boxed up all the pictures we ever took together and put that box in my storage unit. Having the photos somewhere I couldn't see helped keep my memories at bay.

I left that box for a long time. I didn't feel pressured to do anything until I was ready. Eventually, when I felt ready, I opened the box and started to sort through them.

Whatever you decide, I suggest you do some purging, one way or another. Purging can mean deleting photos posted on the internet but keeping hard copies. Or maybe you throw out your wedding photos but keep some photos from the trips you took together. It's really up to you and what you're comfortable with doing.

Engagement Rings and Wedding Bands

For me, jewelry was extremely significant and sentimental; specifically, my engagement ring and wedding band. In my mind, my rings were the biggest symbols of my marriage and unfortunately, my divorce. When I held my rings or even looked at them, a myriad of complex emotions would wash over me. I felt happiness in remembering all the joy and love that had existed between us and the life we once had together. At the same time, my rings also represented the promises we made to one another that had been broken.

My rings also reminded me that life would never be the same. When I looked at them, I felt a lot of grief and remembered all the pain my divorce caused. The best path for me was to rid myself of my jewels because they kept me chained to my past and all I had lost.

Should you do the same? That's really a personal choice. All of it is. Purging anything that is a remnant of your life that once was is a personal choice. Sometimes, it takes a few years to get rid of everything bit by bit; other times, it's as easy as having a massive purge party or burn party with your close friends. If you're anything like me, hanging onto jewelry could be keeping you emotionally and mentally tied to your marriage, your ex, and the past. Even if the ring is tucked away in a drawer and you barely see it or think about it, it's very possible that when you do eventually look at the piece, you'll be reminded of that person and the love that once was. Whether happy or painful, these memories could make it difficult to move on with your life. Looking at your wedding ring could push you to remember all that was right (once upon a time) and could make you relive all that went wrong. The past may have happened a long time ago, but a ring may make a memory feel like it just happened.

If you're still unsure about what to do, maybe you'll appreciate the financial benefit that comes from selling your jewels.

During your divorce, it's very likely you're going to need some extra money. Selling your wedding jewelry will bring cash your way to help with extra costs (like lawyers and movers). Or you can always use extra cash to splurge on something nice for yourself. Maybe it's time for a new wardrobe or a new home that you can decorate exactly like you want. Perhaps you've always dreamed of traveling to Europe but have never been able to afford the trip. Maybe you need a new car. Whatever you've been withholding from yourself becomes more possible if you sell your jewelry and make some extra money.

A divorce is never easy! The healing process can be long and painful. By ridding yourself of things that keep you tied to your past, you are making room in your life for new people, exciting experiences, and beautiful things. Decluttering is a necessary step to help you heal and move forward. You'd be surprised what the universe brings your way once you make room. There's no reason to keep anything that keeps you even remotely tied to your past marriage.

Do yourself a favor and start decluttering to enter your next chapter with an open mind and heart. It's time!

You're Going to Make It.

Your Task

Make a list of everything you need to purge from your life. You can also include ideas of where these items can go (the dump, online marketplace, charity, etc.).

I was meant
to love you, but I was
also meant to evolve
past you.

@thealexandraevamay

THIRTEEN

Decluttering
YOUR LIFE OF EVERYTHING ELSE THAT DOESN'T SERVE YOU

The last chapter discussed things to get rid of after your divorce. If you haven't read that chapter yet, you may want to before you dive into this one, mainly because it can be hard to start the process of letting even little things go, like possessions, never mind big things like friendships. If you start small by getting rid of *things* in your life that no longer serve you, you'll be better equipped to declutter your life of everything else that's either toxic or you have no purpose for.

Let's assume you've read Chapter 12, you've gotten rid of a ton of items, and you're ready for this next step of the decluttering journey.

First, give yourself a big hug for doing what needed to be done with a lot of your things and to give yourself some extra courage for this next part. You're going to be just fine!

Decluttering your life of everything else that doesn't serve you isn't going to be easy. Some of these next steps require you to be extremely brave. But if you can follow through, you will be so much better off! Your life will start opening up beautifully. You will be living much closer to your genuine self. You will be more excited about your life. You will be happier. You will feel more peaceful.

I'm a big believer in energy. If you truly tune into yourself, it can usually be easy to identify when something or someone brings in a dark or heavy energy into your life. The opposite can be said for things and people that make you feel light. If you get silent and really listen to your inner voice, you can usually tell when something is or isn't filling you up.

Have you ever found yourself feeling heavier after an activity? Or "darker," sad, angry, or annoyed? Or have you ever been around someone whose energy feels like a wet blanket? Icky, damp, and lackluster, and it affects your mood and energy too? That's the draining energy I'm talking about. That's what we all need to avoid. If someone or something in your life is making you feel any of these ways, I hope you already have your *declutter aim* focused squarely on this target.

The same can be said for people. There are some people out there who are just draining. They don't necessarily do it intentionally, but it still happens. Sometimes, our personalities just don't mesh with other personalities. It's no one's fault. It just is what it is. There could easily be someone or multiple people in your life right now who are draining your energy. Avoid energy sucks at all costs because they are not what you need, especially at this point in your life when you are on a voyage to rediscover exactly who you are and what you want. Having anyone or anything blocking or draining your energy will get in the way of your journey.

The opposite can be said for anything that makes you feel great or anyone who leaves you feeling uplifted. You deserve to be filled with positivity and light. If someone brings you up, bring them around more often.

After my divorce, I had some decluttering to do in my personal relationships. It was hard, but every step was necessary. It helped with my healing and evolution. It helped me step into my becoming and deepen my awakening. I stopped doing things I didn't love. I switched jobs. I sold my home. I stopped following accounts on social media that made me feel bad about myself. I ended a toxic friendship, and I established boundaries. Not every step was easy, but they were necessary.

Now is the time to take stock of your life and start "cleaning house!"

STOP DOING THINGS YOU DON'T LIKE TO DO

You need to be extremely intentional with your time. You need to fit in hobbies and activities that bring happiness and peace into your life. You should also be making time for self-care and relaxation. Divorce can be mentally and emotionally exhausting, so it's important you build blocks into your week where you can just unwind. Unfortunately, you only have twenty-four hours in a day and so many days in a week. So, you need to prioritize and be intentional.

A big part of being intentional with time is cutting out anything you don't like to do. It can be hard to make time for all the things you love, so why would you waste one minute doing something you don't like? Now is not the time to keep up a class or hobby that you don't enjoy.

Do you truly enjoy that photography class you signed up for? Do you actually like the yoga class you go to every week with your best friend (that you promised you'd go to)? Do you have time for everything? Do you feel like some of your "fun" hobbies have become annoying obligations? Just because you promised once and paid the fee doesn't mean you need to continue doing it in your life.

You do not need to do anything you don't want to do.

Let me repeat.

You do not need to do anything you don't want to do.

It's likely you signed up for the course or made a promise to your friend that you'd commit to a class when you were a less-evolved version of yourself. Life was different then, and so were you. Now that you've started to bloom as your new self, you can change your mind about previous promises made.

You can change your mind. You can quit things. You can say, "Fuck it."

Your friend may be mad in the moment, but she'll get over it. And if she doesn't and holds it against you, is she that much of a friend?

Right now, you need to seek out activities that bring you joy and fill up your life, not hobbies that drain your energy. If something isn't bringing you joy, stop attending. If you don't have the time or energy for something, stop going. Prioritize your wellness and seek out joy in every little corner of your life.

CLEAN UP YOUR SOCIAL MEDIA

We are all guilty of following accounts of people, celebrities, and influencers that make us feel a little bit less great about our own lives. Some examples of accounts you may be following that perhaps you shouldn't be are:

- Cute families that make you feel bad about your divorce.
- Fitness influencers that make you feel bad about your body.

- Moms that only show picture-perfect moments that make you feel bad about yourself as a parent.
- Celebrities who are airbrushed and leave you feeling ugly.
- Successful entrepreneurs who make you feel like you've failed professionally.

We all know that most people on social media only show the *highlight reel* with the very best and brightest moments from their life. But even if you are aware of this fact, the highlight reel from your favorite influencer could be wreaking havoc on your mental health. You may be constantly comparing your life to an unrealistic vision of what you think your own life *should* be. An "unfollow" right now may be the saving grace you need. And you can always follow the account in the future when you're in a better place. Or perhaps you'll never have a desire to follow it again.

Our social media isn't just filled with celebrities and influencers (essentially, strangers on the internet). A huge space on your Instagram and Facebook is probably filled with friends and family, which isn't always the best thing for our mental health. Just because you love someone in person doesn't mean you love what they post online. Maybe their politics don't align with yours and it really gets to you. Maybe the opinions they post are vastly different from yours and you get angry when you read them. There are so many different reasons why someone in your life could get under your skin online.

Someone's internet content is not who they are. It's important we separate the two. We can like someone's personality and not like their content. Consequently, you can love people in real life and not follow them online. You do not need to follow anyone out of obligation. So, take a critical look at your own friend list. Is everyone on the list bringing you happiness? Are you able to fully express yourself without worrying about what your friends think? If not, maybe it's time to make some changes on your page. Some people you may want to unfollow include:

- Friends with different political views.
- Colleagues or friends who make you feel less worthy.
- Family members whose opinions are vastly different from yours.
- Ex-boyfriends or ex-husbands who make you feel sad or angry.
- People who make you feel anxious about posting as your authentic self.
- People who just plain annoy you online.

I am just as guilty as everyone else of following accounts that are bad for me. For example, I followed my ex-husband for months after we split. It was really damaging to my mental health. It made me sad, and I missed him that much more. I couldn't help but silently stalk his page every day, curious about who he was spending time with and what he was doing. It almost became an obsessive act. When we finally unfollowed each other, I set myself free from that madness. I wasn't fully healed, but I felt so much better.

When it comes down to it, it's really important that you only follow accounts, blogs, and pages that spark joy, guidance, or purpose in your life. Sometimes, all it takes is a simple click of the "unfollow" button to achieve the peace we are seeking.

QUIT THAT JOB YOU HATE

This suggestion isn't going to apply to everyone. Some of you may love your job. Maybe it's that one bright spot in your day. If that's the case, then right now is the time to throw yourself into your work. If your work brings you light and happiness, then go for it with all your might and move onto the next parts of this chapter.

Maybe you don't hate your job, but you have settled for it. If that's you, I want you to read this section.

Settling for a job isn't as bad as hating your work, but it still isn't that great. It's kind of like relationships. Sometimes we find ourselves in relationships (or marriages) where we know we're settling, but we stay because we're comfortable, we are scared of letting go of a *sure thing*, or we have no idea how we'd make a change. So, we go with it. For some, this relationship lasts for years and years. I don't want that for you.

I don't want you to just settle for something for years of your life. You deserve so much more than that.

At the same time, I do understand settling for a decent job that pays the bills for the time being. Maybe you've decided that's enough for you, which is, honestly, a very fair decision to make, especially if you need extra money for lawyers, movers, therapists, and everything else that comes up during a divorce. It's easy to say, "Don't settle for a job you don't love." However, at the end of the day, you need work that helps pay the bills. I get it. This very true reality shouldn't be downplayed as not important. Having money doesn't buy happiness but being in debt and having no money can be hard. So, I completely understand working in a job you're just okay with having. And I think that's totally fine, **for now.**

Notice the emphasis on those two words? It's okay to settle *for now*, during this time in your life when you might need extra cash and when so many other things are in transition, but it's not okay to settle long term.

If you are truly just settling in your career, it's important to strive for something more for yourself. The only one who can make your professional dreams a reality is you, so you need to strive for the best for yourself. If right now you're just settling for a job you don't love because it pays the bills, I think there is space to explore other avenues. I'm not saying to quit the job that brings money every month. What I'm saying is to explore other options or opportunities.

Maybe you don't know where to start. That's totally okay. I think a lot of people don't. It's possible you've stayed in this job for so long because you had no idea what else to do.

The first step is to get really quiet and listen to your inner voice. Is there a message you've missed about what you're meant to do? Have you resisted what the universe has been telling you? Have you pushed aside dreams and aspirations because they seem too hard or impossible to achieve?

Every success story starts with the simple decision to go for it. So many successful people don't know exactly how they will get to their end destination, but they make the decision to just start. Then they take it step by step, one goal at a time.

- Do you have a passion that you could turn into an income-earning opportunity?
- Have you always dreamed of starting a side hustle but haven't yet taken the leap?
- Do you look at job postings every month but never apply to any of them?
- Did you study something different in school (that you loved) but settled for a job in a different industry because it was all that was out there at the time for a new grad and now you are still in this industry ten or twenty years later?

- Have you always wanted to go back to school to change careers but never took the leap?

If you answered yes to any of these questions, I think you just found a starting point for a career opportunity. Just by deciding to start, you are on the right track. From here, set small goals to help make this dream a reality. Maybe you can't quit your job just yet, but you can start to make plans. Maybe you could start that side hustle you've been thinking about. Take the plunge and get your toes wet. Who knows where it could lead? If you never try, you'll never know. For some, these initial plans to go after a dream or that side hustle could end up turning into a full-time job one day.

Now, there are some people who truly hate their job or are stuck in unbearably toxic work environments. If that's you, it's really important that you start looking for something else as soon as possible. Going through the devastation of divorce is enough, you don't also need to suffer through a job you hate every day. You deserve so much more.

If a complete career change seems too daunting, perhaps you can look at changing your position within your current company. Or you could apply to your same position with a competitor. A change in scenery may be enough to change your job from one you hate to one you can tolerate. From there, you can start exploring other avenues for work.

We spend so much of our lives working that you may as well do everything in your power to seek out a job that brings you happiness and satisfaction.

It's time to start going after all your dreams!

STAND UP TO DISRESPECTFUL COLLEAGUES (INCLUDING YOUR BOSS)

We already talked about quitting the job you hate, so maybe disrespectful colleagues won't be a problem for much longer. But if you think you'll be in your job for a while, then it's important you have a healthy workplace.

Disrespect from colleagues, managers, supervisors, or bosses can damage your mental health. Everyone deserves to feel safe and respected at work. If you don't feel that way, you need to address the problem. And you are more than strong enough to address it with conviction. You just ended a marriage that didn't serve you. If you haven't fully realized it yet, just through your divorce experience, you've already started your evolution to becoming someone who doesn't take shit from anyone.

I know that standing up to colleagues is different from standing up to your ex, but you have more than enough strength to do it. If you need a bit of extra encouragement to stand up to people in your life (beyond your ex), say these mantras out loud until you believe them:

I am strong.

I am capable.

I am powerful.

I deserve respect.

I deserve to feel safe.

I deserve to be heard.

If you are still feeling hesitant, maybe you aren't 100 percent clear within yourself about what the exact problem is and how to verbalize the issue. The first step is to ask yourself, "What is it about the interactions that make me feel bad?" This question can help you identify where the problem is and verbalize what specifically is bothering you. The more specific you can get about what is affecting you, the better equipped you'll feel to have a conversation.

From here, acknowledge your own fears and insecurities about addressing the problem. Are you scared about being punished for bringing up something? Fearful of repercussions for speaking your truth? Anxious about upsetting someone at work? When you answer these questions and address your fears, you start to feel much better about having a conversation.

Even if it's scary, if someone makes you feel uncomfortable at work or disrespects you constantly, it is time to have a professional conversation and address the problem. If you don't feel comfortable doing it alone, you should ask another colleague or a Human Resources rep to be present. What's the worst thing that will happen if you have this conversation? The best thing, as I see it, is that by having this difficult conversation now, you will save yourself a lot of difficulty in the future and make your workplace a happier place for you. That's definitely worth it!

SELL THAT HOME YOU DON'T LOVE

It's not always easy to part with real estate. First, the financial hit may be really hard on your wallet. After my ex and I split, we sold our house. I lost tens of thousands of dollars on that sale. It fucking sucked, and I was upset for a long time about losing so much money. But eventually, I got back on my feet and made back all the money I lost.

Emotionally, it can also be hard to sell the home, especially if there are a lot of happy memories associated with it. But it is important to keep in mind that memories are just shadows of your past. They don't carve the way for satisfaction in your present or for joy in your future. At the end of the day, even if you have happy memories from the past in the house, if you don't actually love the house, or if it's too expensive to afford every month, or if it's bringing more pain than joy, or if you just want to live somewhere else, it's time to start looking for somewhere new to live.

This same thinking applies to anyone renting a place. If you don't love your rental, get out of it, even if you have to break the lease or don't get your damage deposit back. Your mental health and happiness are more important than any lease. Don't stay stuck somewhere you don't want to be just because of a few minor details.

A new place to live can be the fresh start that you desperately need. A new home can be the fresh canvas you need for all the new memories you're going to make. Even if you don't fully realize it, a new home can be exactly what you need to help you heal and move forward. Your home should be a sanctuary and a haven—rental or owned—so it's time to create and design a space that feels like one, even if it means leaving some money on the table to do so!

STOP HANGING OUT WITH TOXIC FRIENDS

Right now, and always, joy is the goal. It's important that you are doing everything in your power to bring light and healing into your life. You need to do whatever you need to preserve your peace.

Something that can hinder your evolution is anything or anyone toxic that you let take up space in your life. Remember, you are in complete control over who you allow in your life, which includes the friends you choose.

Sometimes, we don't even realize how toxic a friendship really is until we take a step back and reflect. Codependency doesn't just exist exclusively in romantic relationships; it can easily exist in friendships as well. No matter which way you spin it, codependency is never healthy in any type of relationship. Beyond codependency, a friendship may be filled with criticism, passive-aggressive commentary, unhealthy sarcasm, negativity, competition, or judgment. If a friendship has entered this territory or lived in this territory for many years, you've allowed and are continuing to allow dark energy to exist in your life. You don't need it, and you definitely don't deserve it.

We sometimes participate in toxic friendships for years without ever doing anything to address the situation. Maybe you've been friends for decades, possibly since childhood. Maybe you run in the same circle of friends. Maybe you work together. There could be an endless list of reasons that keep you tied to this friendship.

The longevity of a friendship does not obligate you to continue it. If you know that someone isn't good for you, it's important that you create distance from this friendship, something that can be incredibly difficult but incredibly necessary.

One of my favorite quotes is "People enter our lives for a reason, a season, or a lifetime."

It's possible that some of your friends were sent your way for a reason or a season but not for a lifetime. Just because a friendship used to serve you doesn't mean that it necessarily serves you now or in the future as you grow into a more evolved version of yourself. Most people probably agree that it's okay to end an unhealthy relationship or marriage. The same can be said for friendships.

If ending a friendship seems too extreme, you can choose to spend less time with this person or take a mini break from the friendship. You can say no to plans. You don't need to text back. You can take space. It's okay for you to focus on yourself right now.

If you know your friendship is toxic but you aren't wanting to end it or take space, then a difficult conversation may be necessary. It may be time for you to confront the issues and communicate them to your friend. There may be resistance to what you say, but it is also equally possible that this conversation will lead to a breakthrough and lay the groundwork for a better, healthier relationship between the two of you.

If you need help deciding to either end the friendship, take some space, or have a difficult conversation, confide in someone else and ask them for their perspective. You could talk to someone in your family, a different friend, or a therapist. They may have an idea of how to proceed. Ultimately, the decision will be yours, but another perspective may help you understand the situation better.

Remember that you deserve light and happiness in all areas of your life, which includes friendships. Don't settle for less than you deserve!

SET BOUNDARIES WITH YOUR FAMILY

Sometimes, family members can be the biggest roadblocks on our journey to attain personal fulfillment, happiness, or growth. Whether intentional or not, family members can subtly or overtly protest our evolution. It isn't typically done maliciously. Most family members do things and say things out of a place of love and care. Even so, intention and execution are entirely different things.

For example, your mom might be telling you to fix your marriage. Or maybe your dad is telling you that being a single parent will be too hard. Maybe your sister has been showing up at your house every night "just to make sure you're okay." Maybe your brother has been sending your ex mean messages on Facebook. All these examples are actions committed out of love for you, but they aren't necessarily all that supportive or healthy.

I know it can be difficult, but boundaries are necessary. They are healthy for both you and the other party. Your family will never know when they overstep boundaries if you don't communicate what your boundaries are. You owe it to yourself, and you owe it to them. By establishing boundaries, you are prioritizing something that needs to be a priority in your life: your mental health.

Hopefully, your family responds positively to your boundaries. If they don't, continue to communicate what you need until it sinks in. It's okay to say something more than once. It's okay to say something over and over. It's also okay to take some space until boundaries are respected.

Boundaries are sometimes the most loving gift you can give yourself.

You're Going to Make It.

Your Task

Make a list of the things that don't serve you or your growth. For each thing, write down the steps you will take to remove it from your life.

Loving yourself
is the most important
thing you'll ever do.

@thealexandraevamay

FOURTEEN

Dating
AFTER DIVORCE AND TRUSTING AGAIN

When I started writing this book, I wasn't sure if I wanted to include anything about dating. I wanted to focus on healing after divorce, and I don't think that necessarily includes dating. But for some of us, dating can be part of the healing process and can help ease the shift from being married to the next chapter. Ideally, you should build confidence and self-esteem all on your own; however, if it doesn't happen organically, getting out there and dating again can be the one thing that reminds us we aren't broken, love can happen again, and there are plenty of available people who are worthy of dating.

If you've even contemplated dating, give yourself a huge hug. Going from ending a marriage to a place where dating has entered your mind is a long process. So, if you're at the point where you're considering the possibility of dating, you've gotten through a bunch of hard times already. Your journey up until here, and the strength you've demonstrated, is nothing short of amazing. Please hold this truth in your heart.

After divorce, many people seek out a second chance at love through new relationships. Some of us even go on to remarry and take another shot at lifelong commitment. I think it's safe to say that even after the destruction of divorce, many of us haven't given up hope that love is possible or that a different marriage could be better. There are a lot of divorcées I've spoken with who have told me it wasn't the institution of marriage that let them down, it was the relationship within the institution that crumbled.

Just because one marriage fails, many of us know, deep in our gut, that a different relationship or a different marriage could be incredible.

During the pain of divorce, we do what we need to protect ourselves. We build walls around our hearts that aren't easy to take down. When you start dating, it's normal to have your guard up and to not let anyone past your walls. It's normal to have fears about the unknown. It's natural to experience anxiety over the idea that another relationship or marriage could fail.

It's also normal to be hypervigilant about certain things that have hurt you in the past. If your ex cheated on you, it's natural to feel like someone else might do the same thing. If your ex was abusive, it's normal to be looking for the signs it could happen again. If your ex left you, you may feel like any love interest in the future will do the exact same thing. All these behaviors happen because our mind is trying to protect our heart from the pain and trauma we've experienced before.

If you're feeling this way, be gentle with yourself. You're human. After divorce, feeling uneasy about dating is human.

It took me a while to feel ready to date. Honestly, it wasn't something I had really experienced. Before getting married, I was a *relationship girl*. I moved from one relationship to another. I hadn't experienced dating and wasn't prepared for what it was like. At first, I was scared. I had no idea what to expect and didn't really know what kind of people were out there. I'm happy I moved through that fear.

Did it go smoothly? No way! I had horrible dates, awkward situations, and wrong matches. I dated liars, cheats, immature men, and men who only wanted one thing.

Unknowingly, I even went on a date with a guy who was awaiting trial for manslaughter, something I didn't know at first. Before meeting him, I just thought he was a nice guy who was pretty cute.

And where did I meet this stand-up gentleman, you ask? Exactly where I met so many other "gems"—online. We struck up quite the connection over Tinder. We chatted for a few weeks before meeting, which is kind of rare. Because we had been chatting for a while and quite consistently, I was excited for our first date. And the first date didn't disappoint. At least, not at first.

He had booked reservations at a nice restaurant, dressed up, and even had a gift for me. If I remember correctly, it was tea and an air plant. It was really thoughtful. We ended up having a date that lasted well over three hours, chatting the whole time. By the end of the date, I was starting to like the guy, feeling all those good butterflies. And that's the exact moment he said, "So, I have a bit of a bomb to drop . . . "

If a man on a date ever utters any statement about dropping bombs, nothing good will follow.

He then proceeded to tell me about what had happened and his upcoming trial. I tried my best to keep my face neutral through his story, but I'm sure my shock at the whole situation was plain as day. The saving grace in this situation was that he at least told me about it. He said he told me "because I looked like a nice person who deserved to know."

Let's get one thing straight—honesty about criminal charges isn't something you reserve just for *nice* people. That's the kind of thing you should divulge to *any* person. Arguably, you should also refrain from dating if you're awaiting trial, but I guess we all have our own ideas about how dating should go.

Either way, unfortunately for him, conjugal visits aren't my jam, and neither was a second date.

About a year after the date, I googled him. He had been found guilty and had to serve time. From this experience, I learned some very valuable lessons.

First off, google everyone *before* you agree to a date. Or give one of your best friends this job. Trust me, there is someone in your friend group who could work for the FBI with their level of stalking abilities online. If I had gotten this guy's last name before the first date and had searched him online (or had my best friend search him), I would have had about twenty articles to read about his upcoming trial. Second, if you do by chance unknowingly happen to go out with your very own criminal, try to have faith that not all men actually commit manslaughter. And if you have bad dates, do your best not to lose hope that there are good ones out there.

As you can imagine, my experience on this particular date made it somewhat difficult to keep my head up.

Honestly, I lost hope during the dating process a lot. I let all the failed dates and bad matches get to me. I got super down about the whole *dating game.* I got to a point where I didn't think I would ever find love again.

If you're in a stage of hopelessness, please know you're in good company. At the same time, holding yourself back from the possibility of a relationship due to fear is cheating yourself out of what could be the love of your life.

I'm so happy I moved through any fear and hopelessness I was feeling because I learned a lot from dating and from the people I met along the way. Now, I want to pass these lessons on to you.

MAKE SURE YOU'RE TRULY READY

In all honesty, I started dating too soon and should have waited longer. I started dating quickly after my split for a couple of reasons. I thought I had missed out on the *dating stage*. As I mentioned, I had always been a relationship girl. Before my marriage, I had jumped from one relationship to the next. I never had a period of time in my life to date a bunch of people and just have fun with it. I think this reason was why I started dating so quickly after my marriage ended. I wanted to experience what I thought I had missed out on. I also think I was filling a void and searching for something. My understanding of who I was when I was married was very much enmeshed in my identity as being part of a couple. When that part of me came to an end, I was lost. Choosing to date quickly after the split was my attempt to regain that piece of me that felt lost.

In reflection, I should have worked on finding myself instead of looking for someone else to help me understand who I was. I should have worked on loving myself instead of looking to get love from someone else.

I also really wanted children. I didn't have children in my first marriage and was terrified that if I waited too long, I would either not be able to have kids because of my age or never find a suitable man with whom to raise children. I now know this was an incredibly unhealthy reason to pursue dating.

I'm happy to say that I've come to a place in my life where I will never again use that desire as a reason to seek out a relationship. Dating isn't about finding a father for your future kids, it's about finding someone who is going to be an amazing addition to your life (even if kids aren't part of that equation).

Despite it all, dating ended up being an important part of my healing journey. My divorce had put me through the emotional ringer, and my self-esteem was at an all-time low, so just getting out there again and experiencing the interest of men affirmed for me that I wouldn't be alone forever and that I was desirable, wanted, and lovable, something that provided a lot of comfort during a time I felt so low. But I should have waited a lot longer before dipping my toes into the dating world. Either way, it's in the past and is very much part of my journey.

No one, except for you, is going to know when you're ready to date. A word of advice: If you know you aren't ready, there's no rush!

Take as much time as you need. Work on yourself first and make sure you're healed. Any brokenness you still feel could affect the success of your dates or possible relationships. Worse, dating too soon could result in you waking up years later realizing that you still don't know who you are and that there are wounds left to heal.

If you know you aren't ready to date, don't take offense when friends and family encourage you to get back out there. Nobody knows what is right for you except for you. Don't feel pressured to date too soon just because someone else thinks it's good for you. Make dating choices based on what you know is best for you.

KNOW YOUR GOALS BEFORE YOU START DATING

To avoid leading anyone on, breaking hearts, or worst of all, having your heart broken, it's important to know your dating goals before you get out there. Be real with yourself. Maybe you just started dating and all you're looking for is casual dates and some fun. Maybe you want to date just a few people or lots of people at the same time. Maybe you have no idea what type of person you eventually want to settle down with and right now you just want to get to know who's out there. That is more than okay!

It's important you know your intentions for dating. Be real with yourself and anyone you date. Are you dating for fun? Connection?

Love? Commitment? A relationship? If you have a clear idea of what you're looking to get out of dating, you're less likely to be disappointed. If you have a clear goal in mind, hopefully you won't end up dating people who don't have the same goal as you. Do yourself a favor and only date people who want the same thing as you. Listen to what a potential match says about their goals. If their goals differ from yours, don't assume they will ever want what you want.

If you are looking for love and a long-term commitment, you need to be honest about it with both yourself and the people you date. Some of us will try to *play it cool* and claim we are okay with a casual fling with the hope the other person will fall for us and change their mind. That rarely happens. If, in the beginning, someone says that all they want is something casual, believe them. If you are looking for love and commitment, only date people who are also looking for that. If you know you're looking to date to get married but the person you're with doesn't want that type of relationship, don't assume they'll ever change their mind or that your love will alter what they want. If you want kids and they don't, it's very unlikely they'll switch their stance. Exceptions exist, but they're rare.

At the same time, if you don't want a relationship, it's not fair to lead others along who are looking for one. Don't get mixed up with someone who's looking for much more than you can offer right now. Only date people who are looking for the same things from dating that you are.

IF YOU'RE LOOKING FOR COMMITMENT, KNOW WHAT YOU NEED IN A PARTNER

Be realistic with yourself about the type of partner you want long term. When I started dating, I was pretty lost. I confused what I *wanted* in someone with what I *needed* in a partner, which is the OPPOSITE of what you should do. It's so important for you to differentiate your needs and wants when it comes to what you're looking for in a future relationship. What you want in a partner may also be what you need; however, what you need is sometimes outside of the scope of what you want.

When I was lost, what helped me was to make a long list of all the qualities I was looking for in a man. This list included absolutely every little quality I hoped to find. I went through the list and circled my "must-haves." I wanted a man who was smart and funny, but it wasn't a need, mainly because my ex was both extremely smart and very funny, and I still ended up divorced. Reflecting on all the ways my first marriage didn't serve me, I realized that what I needed, more than a smart and funny partner, was a man who is kind and empathetic and who prioritizes our relationship. If I was dating someone, and he was both smart and funny but demonstrated a lack of empathy or didn't make me a priority, I said good-bye. My want for a smart, funny guy will always be trumped by my need for a kind man. You may want a man who is tall with muscles, but that might just be a hopeful wish. A must-have is a quality you can't live without.

KNOW THAT YOU DESERVE TO BE TREATED WELL

People approach dating in different ways post-divorce. Some people have it figured out and don't settle for any nonsense. These people are my heroes, and I'm truly in awe of their confidence! At the same time, there's a lot of people who will settle for anyone who throws them a second glance. They've been through so much and they just want to feel desired, pursued, and loved. They yearn to feel close to someone. They want the dream.

I understand how easy it is to fall into this category because I was there. Early on, when I was just starting to date after my divorce, every guy who showed me even a scrap of interest was given a place in my heart. I wanted to be in love again, and I was used to the serious commitment of marriage. Dating *just for fun* wasn't in my scope of understanding.

Unfortunately, I got wrapped up in men who hadn't earned that type of attention. A lot of these guys hadn't shown me that they appreciated me or valued me. Yet, there I was, giving them my time, attention, and feelings. These connections blew up in my face. Either the guy wasn't right for me, or I wasn't right for the guy. If I had approached dating differently from the start, I could have avoided disappointment and self-doubt.

The turning point came for me when I realized that I deserved to be valued, appreciated, and treated well. I deserved more than bread-crumbs over dating apps. I deserved more than men who didn't call or text back. I deserved more than men who could go weeks without a second or third date. I deserved more than men who were emotionally unavailable. Once this realization came to me, I approached dating much differently. I didn't beat myself up if something didn't work out. I didn't get involved too soon. If I felt like I was being mistreated, I could easily walk away because I wasn't invested.

I also developed authentic, healthy connections with men who were interested in a real way and made me a priority. I only made time for those who treated me the way I deserved.

MANAGE YOUR EXPECTATIONS

Early on, I had been going about dating all wrong! I had huge expectations when I barely knew the person. I imagined futures with people when I didn't even know their last name, which is something you should not do. One of the best things I did for myself was start to change my expectations about any potential love interest.

If you decide to go on a first date with someone, keep your expectations low. If you manage your expectations, I promise you that you'll feel less disappointed. Go on the date with only the hope that you'll have some good conversation and fun. That's it. Don't expect a beautiful future. Don't even expect a second date. If those things happen, great! However, don't set yourself up to be disappointed if they don't.

During the first few dates, don't be too quick to stop talking to and meeting other people. In the beginning, you're just getting to know people and are free to date others. There were quite a few times when I got too invested too quickly and stopped seeing or talking to everyone else, only to find myself ghosted. Then, I was disappointed that I had ended things with other nice people for someone who hadn't earned my undivided attention yet. They hadn't earned it because we had only been out two times! Until you have the conversation that you're exclusive, you're free to date other people and keep your options open, something that will also help you avoid heartbreak in case someone ends it after a few dates.

When you first start dating someone, you don't owe them your love or attention. Just because you've been chatting online for a few weeks and have been out on one or two dates with a potential match doesn't mean you owe them a future. After the initial stages of getting to know someone, you may decide the person isn't for you, which is 100 percent fine. Some people may take it personally and respond with anger; however, most people are understanding. If someone gets mad at you for ending the relationship, that's not your problem. You'll quickly develop a thick skin.

Just as important is to keep in mind that anyone you date early on is probably also getting to know lots of other people. Just like you don't owe anyone anything at this point, no one owes you anything either. You can't be upset if they are chatting with others before you have a conversation about commitment. Even if someone takes you on a date every week, messages you "good morning" and "good night" every day for a month or calls you every day, never lose sight of the fact that they could easily be doing that with other people. If you're cognizant of this fact, you hopefully won't get too invested in someone during the early stages before they have earned that investment. The early part is just about getting to know someone, sharing some witty banter, and having some fun.

Don't catch feelings too soon!

KEEP YOUR STANDARDS HIGH

Even if you've been burned by divorce, please know you deserve the world.

With that in mind, always keep your standards high. Trust that you deserve everything you dream of for yourself. Know what you want and what you deserve and don't settle for less. If someone doesn't meet your standards, then you know what you need to do. If you have to say good-bye to someone and you've managed your expectations, then your heart won't be too damaged. You'll be able to say good-bye and move on easily and quickly.

When setting standards, a lot of people place a great deal of importance and expectations on what someone says, something that may set you up for failure. Someone may say wonderful things to you on your dates and text you every day, all day, continuing to say the most wonderful compliments. These words can be intoxicating and easy to fall for; however, if their actions don't match up, their words mean absolutely nothing. If someone is saying wonderful things to you all the time, yet they aren't making the effort to see you, these words mean nothing. At the same time, if someone is seeing you yet not saying anything to make you feel special, then actions don't mean much either.

It's important to always consider words and actions together, never just one or the other.

BE HONEST ABOUT YOUR EX AND YOUR KIDS . . . BUT NOT TOO HONEST, TOO SOON

I know someone who insisted on including his kids in all the pictures that he posted on his online dating profiles. He wanted to make sure everyone knew that his children were his number one priority. This behavior is extremely admirable and identifies the type of person that many people want to date. So why didn't he get many matches? Why were women hesitant to message him? It was because he was *too* honest, *too* soon. Yes, there is such a thing as being too honest and open too soon. Should he have lied about having kids? Of course not. Should he have completely refrained from posting pictures of his kids? Not necessarily; however, there's a balance.

The people interested in dating you need to get to know you before they get to know your kids. You need to present yourself first. By presenting your entire family in such an upfront way, you could easily scare someone away. This theory applies to all family members. When I was dating, I wasn't posting photos of my sister, brother, or parents. They are my family and that information would be shared once someone earned it, just like information about your kids should only be shared once someone earns that information. It's intimidating to others to have all the information about your family upfront. They are just starting to feel you out. Let them do that without the pressure of kids.

This advice also applies to any information you offer about your ex. When you are dating, you can mention that you share custody with your ex or that you were married and you don't speak with your ex anymore, but leave it at that. You don't need to explain why you split or go into the nitty-gritty details about how your ex is awful. If your relationship develops with someone, all this information will eventually come out. In the beginning, keep it off the table. Focus on the new relationship you're developing and not the relationship you used to have.

TRY NOT TO HAUL IN YOUR PAST BAGGAGE

When you're on a date and you're nervous, it's super easy to go off on a tangent about how your ex did you wrong. But trust me when I say that romantic interests don't want to hear about your baggage with your ex or the dirty details about your divorce (even if they went through a divorce themselves). That information should be reserved for your friends and family.

Maybe down the line if you develop a relationship with someone, you'll share some of your past baggage with them; however, do your best to keep that to a limit as well. Sometimes, bringing up old baggage can make the person on the receiving end feel like they are being compared to a ghost from the past. No one wants to feel like that. Even if you've been dating someone for months, or years, they aren't your ex and don't necessarily need to hear all about your past relationship or your former spouse. They aren't the person responsible for your baggage, so don't make it their job to carry your stuff. Instead, focus on the relationship you are building with them and let the past stay in the past.

THE PEOPLE YOU DATE ARE <u>NOT</u> YOUR EX

Even if your new love interest resembles your ex and reminds you of them, they are not your ex. The way they react to certain situations may differ completely from the way your ex behaved. They may approach conflict differently. The way they spend their free time may be different from what your ex enjoyed doing. Maybe their idea of a romantic date is completely different from what you're used to. Maybe their love language is different. Nearly everything about your new love interest may be different, so treat the person as such. Approach each person you date with fresh eyes and an open mind. Try your best not to set someone else up to fail by having certain expectations. Judge them for them and not for anything your ex did. Don't punish new love interests for the sins of your ex. If, for example, your ex cheated on you and you have serious trust issues, your new person should not take the brunt of your trust issues. If your ex used to always cancel plans at the last minute and your new love interest cancels once, don't assume it will be their pattern just because it was your ex's tendency.

Anyone who's been through heartbreak can be guilty of being hypervigilant, but it can work against you and ruin your chances of establishing a genuine connection with an amazing person. Give people the benefit of the doubt and assume good intentions unless they give you a reason to doubt them, of course. There are good people out there. You just might have to kiss a few frogs or slay a few dragons first.

ALLOW YOURSELF TO TRUST AGAIN

I'm not an expert in building up trust, I only know what I experienced. For a long time, I had a difficult time trusting anyone. My ex never cheated, but he hurt me deeply. Unfortunately, I believed every man would hurt me in the same manner. Even if I told myself I could trust someone, there was a voice in the back of my mind that told me I would get hurt. It was really hard to quiet this voice.

I think my turning point was not the decision to trust again but rather the decision to let go of any control I thought I had over anyone else's behavior.

I surrendered to the reality that I could only control myself. How other people chose to behave was more about them, and it didn't mean anything about me.

If someone was going to hurt me, they were going to do it whether I trusted them or not. I had no control over their decision to treat me with respect and kindness. By relinquishing the control I thought I had, I was able to attain a level of peace and acceptance that I hadn't felt before. I couldn't control whether someone hurt me in the future, so why stress over it?

Eventually, I decided to give people the benefit of the doubt. It no longer made sense to take myself down the rabbit hole of trust issues with anyone who hadn't given me a reason not to trust them.

I also figured that if someone hurt me, it wasn't anything I couldn't handle. I had become a badass survivor after my divorce, so I figured there wouldn't be anything that could hurt me the way divorce had destroyed me. If someone in my future does manage to hurt me more than my divorce did, I've come to a place where I can finally say with full confidence that any hurt from a relationship is meant to teach me something and is an important part of my journey.

Dating after divorce can be hard. If you get discouraged, reflect on how far you've already come. Don't get upset about any dating "failures." Rather, be proud of the wins and the fact that you're putting yourself out there. You've been through enough—you don't need to waste time being upset or spend time with people who don't deserve you. Right now, I hope you are filled with newfound confidence and have made the promise to yourself that you won't settle for anything short of extraordinary.

You deserve every beautiful thing you've always dreamed of!

You're Going to Make It.

Your Task

Before you dip your toes into the dating world, it's not only important to reflect on where you've been and mistakes you've made in the past but also on where you want to go from here.

Some questions for you to explore:

- What red flags have you missed in past partners?
- What do you want to look out for in the future?
- What will you NOT accept from future partners?
- How have you lost yourself in past relationships?
- How did your marriage NOT serve you?
- How can you grow as a potential partner for someone?

From there, reflect on what you're looking for:

- What are your dating goals?
- What qualities are you looking for in an ideal partner?
- What are your must-have qualities?
- In your ideal world, what would a romantic relationship look like?

Fulfilling, reciprocal, profound love exists. Don't settle for scraps.

FIFTEEN

Walking
PROUDLY INTO YOUR FUTURE

Somewhere in the darkness of my divorce was the push to not only survive but to thrive. Somewhere in there, a desire to be unapologetically myself—a woman who led a life filled with passion, pleasure, joy, adventure, fun, love, and peace—awakened. And somewhere in that darkness, I realized that I was capable of being someone who lived her life consciously with intention and that I desired a conscious, healthy partnership where we evolved together and propelled each other forward.

Divorce changes everything and completely shifts your world. When you're eventually able to pull yourself up off the floor, things will be different. Transformation is inevitable. Weakness will be replaced with strength. Resiliency becomes second nature and hope fills your soul.

You will probably be a completely different person than who you were before everything fell apart. And that's more than okay.

I used to be a people-pleaser who sacrificed parts of myself to make others happy. I didn't have the internal strength necessary to prioritize my happiness or mental health. I didn't establish necessary boundaries in relationships or friendships. I sacrificed my happiness ALL the time to make others happy. My life at that time was a result or direct consequence of me catering to everyone else's needs, desires, and wishes, while dimming my own.

I was also in a marriage that didn't serve me and wouldn't serve me long term. I didn't realize it for the majority of the relationship, but when I eventually woke up to this truth, I was able to make peace with my journey. I don't hold any ill will toward my ex-husband. I do truly wish him well and hope he's happy. I'm thankful for the relationship and for the impact he had on my life. We had amazing times together; we were in love, and we shared a lot. He will always hold a special place in my heart, but I know we are meant to walk two separate paths. The marriage was destined to end. We were meant to live this life without each other.

When I finally emerged from my divorce, I was a completely different version of myself. From the ashes of ruin were the pieces necessary for transformation. Divorce was the experience that I desperately needed to wake me up! It was what I needed to transform and finally discover who I really am.

Everything's different now. I'm different. I've evolved. I've awakened, and I don't ever plan on going backward. The only way up, is up.

> Life after divorce happened.
>
> I moved forward.
>
> Let go.
>
> Healed.
>
> Changed.

I'm much clearer about who I am, about what I want, and about what I deserve. I establish boundaries. I say no and don't feel guilty about "disappointing" anyone. I do what's right for me, I take care of my mental health, and I prioritize my happiness. I love myself exactly as I am, no matter what hardships or struggles come my way. I never would have become the woman I am today if I hadn't suffered through my divorce.

How can I regret one moment of my pain if it has led me to a deeper understanding of myself? The answer is simple: I can't.

My life has also changed in a beautiful way, which happened because I trusted the universe to bring things my way at the right time. And the universe answered this trust with so many blessings. I've had incredible experiences since my split and have met wonderful people. My life has fallen into place exactly as it was meant to.

As mentioned, one of my dreams was to travel. So, I made that happen. I bought the tickets, boarded the plane, and found myself on the other side of the world . . . a few times. I traveled through Portugal and Spain with my sister, where I spent four weeks exploring foreign cities, suntanning on beaches, and drinking local wine. I traveled solo through Greece, where I visited the Parthenon, partied until 5:00 in the morning, and met a lifelong friend. I also traveled to Bolivia and Peru and explored South America with my best friends. We ate at one of Anthony Bourdain's favorite restaurants, stayed in hostels, visited a floating village, and spent four days hiking the Inca Trail, which ended up being one of the most challenging physical feats of my entire life.

More than just travel, I also achieved financial independence, moved downtown, lived with my best friend, got to know myself, took my health seriously, met amazing people, dated, opened my broken heart, pursued love, became a mother, and wrote like my life depended on it.

Everything combined has led me here to finishing this book. Trust me when I say that writing a book isn't an easy feat; however, it was one of my biggest dreams, so there wasn't room for any excuse that might have gotten in the way. I worked away at it, night after night, week after week, and year after year. Every chapter was a challenge and had me crying all the tears, but every word was worth it because eventually, I found myself here: writing the last chapter of this book that has become so dear to my heart.

The path that formed after the end of my marriage NEVER would have happened without my divorce. It had to happen at exactly the time it happened. I wasn't meant to stay married. My destiny depended on it. Divorce carved out a path that has led to an extraordinary journey. I honestly have no idea what the future holds, but I'm certain that it will be beautiful, bright, messy, complex, and extraordinary. My wish is for you to find the same joy and peace that I have found and for you to never shy away from the hard stuff, the heart-wrenching stuff that will tear you apart so you can become who you were destined to be. Never shy away from a lifetime of adventure, love, joy, and anything else you desire. Never, ever settle—in love, marriage, friendships, or your career. Hold your standards high! Everything and everyone will either rise to meet you there or fall away organically.

And if you know deep down in your heart of hearts that you're stuck in an unhealthy, toxic marriage or partnership but don't have the courage to leave just yet, I see you. My wish for you is to find the courage to leave, and if you need a little help doing so, pray to whatever higher power you believe in to take away the toxicity. I promise it works. I'm living proof. You have a beautiful life ahead of you—don't waste away in a relationship that doesn't fulfill you, bring you love, peace, and joy, or treat you with respect.

And that's the thing with divorce. Everything is uncertain, and you don't really know what the future holds. That uncertainty can be scary, and the pain can seem unbearable. But it can also be wonderful.

For me, even with all the fear and all the pain, it's still been spectacular because somehow, I landed here. And here is magic.

During your own grief and healing, don't lose sight of what could be. Even in the darkness, hold onto the light you want for yourself. Because you never know where you will land, and you never know what magic is waiting for you. You've been given a phenomenal gift from the universe—the gift of starting over and creating the life of your dreams. It's not very often that you get this opportunity. Don't waste it!

Now is the time, more than ever, for you to be 100 percent true to yourself. You're experiencing an incredibly transformative shift that has the potential to lead you to the life you've always dreamed about. Everything you've ever imagined can happen for you. It's all possible.

Your awakening is here!

Take time to reflect on what you truly want, and not what you think you want or what society tells you that you want (like a relationship and getting married again). Then go after it with full conviction. There's nothing holding you back from creating the life of your dreams.

Have you been living in the suburbs for your whole married life but always wanted to live downtown in a loft-style condo? Well, it's time to start looking at condos. Have you always wanted to try photography but never had the time or money? Start saving money and create a plan to make space in your life for the photography class. Have you wanted to change careers or go back to school? Now is the time to take the leap and change your life.

While you're reflecting on what you want in your life, be honest with yourself about what you need and what will bring you joy. You've been through enough pain and grief. You owe it to yourself to seek out exactly what is right for you.

> *You owe yourself more than just happiness; you owe yourself joy.*

If that's a yoga class every other night, then take the damn yoga class every other night. If joy is an annual trip to Mexico to lie on a beach and drink margaritas, then book your ticket and get yourself on a plane every year to enjoy the beach and drink those margaritas. If joy is simply spending every Sunday relaxing on the couch watching your favorite shows, then make time for that every week. Or if joy is starting a side hustle or business, go do it. Devote yourself to it! There should be nothing standing in your way. If there is, get rid of whatever or whoever is blocking you from achieving joy.

If you are ready (and wanting) to start dating again, be honest with yourself about what you want and what you deserve. If you want to have a fling, then have a fling. If you are looking for love and commitment, then don't settle for anyone who isn't also looking for that. Be real about your standards. Establish healthy boundaries and don't settle!

It's time to go after *all* your dreams. This is your chance to create the life you've always wanted. Have faith that you can make it all happen, set goals for yourself, and, most importantly, act on your goals to make your dreams a reality.

This next chapter in your life has endless possibilities. Anything is possible. You are worthy of everything. There are no limits. Go after it all.

You deserve the fiercely beautiful life you dream about.

So get out there and make it happen!

Wishing you

only peace and light. Always.

If the story ends, the best way to move on is picking up a new book and starting a new chapter.

ABOUT THE AUTHOR

Alexandra Eva-May is a writer, blogger, motivational speaker, mental health advocate, and divorcée who is on a mission to help others on their healing journey after divorce. You can often find her on her blog or Instagram, sharing how she healed from her own split. She is in constant pursuit of peace, light, and happiness and works to motivate others to seek the same.

When she's not writing, Alexandra spends most of her time reading, bike riding, going to the mountains, being by the water, traveling the world, exploring home renovation blogs, and tasting wine. As a new mother, she is currently living on endless cups of coffee. She was born and raised in Alberta, Canada, and lives there to this day with her partner and son.

Connect with her at www.thesplendidpath.com or say hi to her on Instagram @thealexandraevamay

REFERENCED RESOURCES

CHAPTER 2

Murphy, Ryan, dir. *Eat Pray Love*. 2010. Sony Pictures Entertainment.

CHAPTER 3

Lesser, Elizabeth. *Broken Open: How Difficult Times Can Help Us Grow*. Reprint. Villard, 2005.

Chödrön, Pema. *Living Beautifully with Uncertainty and Change*. Shambhala, 2012.

CHAPTER 6

1. Abrams, Allison. "Post-Divorce Trauma and PTSD." *VeryWell Mind*, July 9, 2021. https://www.verywellmind.com/post-divorce-trauma-4583824

2. "Sour mood getting you down? Get back to nature." *Harvard Health Publishing*, March 30, 2021. https://www.health.harvard.edu/mind-and-mood/sour-mood-getting-you-down-get-back-to-nature (accessed September 26, 2021.)

"A Potential Natural Treatment for Attention-Deficit/Hyperactivity Disorder: Evidence from a National Study." *NCBI*, September 2004. https://www.ncbi.nlm.nih.gov/pmc/articles/PMC1448497/ (accessed September 26, 2021.)

University Of Illinois at Urbana-Champaign. "Children With ADHD Benefit from Time Outdoors Enjoying Nature." *ScienceDaily*. www.sciencedaily.com/releases/2004/08/040830082535.htm (accessed September 26, 2021).

Maté, Gabor. *When the Body Says No: The Cost of Hidden Stress*. Random House of Canada, 2004.

CHAPTER 7

Fogelman, Dan, creator. *This Is Us*. 20th Television (2016–2020); Disney–ABC Domestic Television (2020–present).

YGTMedia Co. is a blended boutique publishing house for mission-driven humans. We help seasoned and emerging authors "birth their brain babies" through a supportive and collaborative approach. Specializing in narrative nonfiction and adult and children's empowerment books, we believe that words can change the world, and we intend to do so one book at a time.

🌐 ygtmedia.co/publishing

📷 @ygtmedia.co

f @ygtmedia.co